CW00840122

SOC]

How forward-thinking B2B's can unleash the power of social media

ANDY LAMBERT

Copyright © 2022 Andy Lambert

www.andyrlambert.com

DEDICATION

To my wonderful family, Natalie, Henry and Freddie. Without their support none of this would have been possible.

ACKNOWLEDGMENTS

Thank you to all of the wonderful ContentCal customers that have shown us incredible support and taught me so much over the years.

Thank you to Colin Smith for being an incredible mentor, wonderful friend and for introducing me to Alex Packham, CEO and Founder of ContentCal.

Meeting Alex has transformed my professional life and is one of those entrepreneurs that you just know is going on to do even more remarkable things. Thank you also to Tom Hopkins for giving me the push I needed to write this book.

Finally, thank you to Philip Robinson who lit the fire of entrepreneurship in me. An incredible man and a huge inspiration. Rest in peace. You'll be forever remembered.

BACKGROUND

My career started in sales. As with any salesperson you're always looking at ways to maximise leverage and find ways of achieving maximum results with minimum effort. This was 2012, and Twitter was gaining significant traction in the UK. I saw Twitter as an opportunity to tap into people's conversations at scale, using its incredible listening power to my sales advantage. However, 10 years later, in 2022, whilst the term 'social selling' has now become commonplace, the practice is still underutilised.

At the same time, LinkedIn was also beginning to gain traction. I saw this as an opportunity to demonstrate my understanding of the category, using the content I was creating as a way to start conversations with prospects. We now call this practice 'employee advocacy', but yet again, very few B2B's have truly unlocked the potential of this.

Roll the clock forward a few years and in 2016 I became one of the founders of ContentCal, a social media management software, aimed at helping businesses of any size unlock the power of social media.

We launched ContentCal at the beginning of 2017, and over the course of four years, scaled to over 3,500 customers in more than 100 countries.

The majority of this growth was driven through content marketing and a huge proportion of this was as a result of our work on social media. In 2021 alone, over 15,000 people had joined our webinars and more than 40,000 people had downloaded at least one piece of our educational content.

The end of 2021, ContentCal was acquired by Adobe. Adobe understood the opportunity afforded by social media and saw this as the perfect chance to bring social media planning and publishing tools to their millions of customers.

Over the course of the last 6 years at ContentCal, from the creation of the business to the sale to Adobe we've helped thousands of businesses unlock the power of social media, but we've also seen the challenges first-hand and have learned the hard way what does and does not work.

I'll be sharing some examples over the course of this book, but the thing that became abundantly clear to me over the course of our journey at ContentCal is both the unprecedented power of social media but also how far behind the majority of B2B businesses are.

My hope for this book is that it all serves as a source of inspiration for B2B businesses that have yet to realise the transformative power of social media.

I hope you enjoy it.

Andy

INTRODUCTION

Social media is undergoing one of the biggest macro shifts in its history. Worldwide adoption of social media platforms grew by 10% from 2021 to 2022, meaning over 500 million new users began logging in to social media platforms on a monthly basis.

The balance has now been tipped. Over half (58%) of the worlds' population, or 4.6 billion people, to put it another way, are now logging in to social platforms every single month.

This growth of social media adoption has led to another macro shift in user behaviour. Over 43% of users now turn to social media as a primary channel to discover new products and services, according to Global Web Index and Visa also estimate that 1 in 4 of all product purchases are influenced by social media.

This purchase intent is powering the dawn of 'social commerce'. Social media platforms are falling over themselves to release features that capture users' latent demand to spend money. As a result, we've seen the release of Instagram, Facebook and Pinterest Shops, giving users an opportunity to purchase products without leaving the platforms, along with the latest growth area of live-streamed e-commerce.

This shift to social commerce is at the same time powering the growth of the 'creator economy' - of which we'll explore in greater detail later in this book - which is creating microcosms of niche communities, all with their own unique subcultures.

These macro shifts represent an incredible opportunity for businesses - but tapping into them won't be easy.

Especially so, when we consider how emerging technologies like Augmented Reality, the Metaverse and Web3 will impact how we approach social media - and you begin to realise that most businesses are ill-equipped to maximise this opportunity.

None more so than B2B businesses.

In my experience, B2B's have been the most guilty of seeing social media as just another 'channel', and have approached it in the same way they would an email list - pumping out an endless stream of self-serving content and wondering why the results are nowhere to be seen.

In my view, there are four core factors that prevent many B2B's from creating a successful social media strategy;

1. The obsession with short term ROI.

B2B's are on the monthly/quarterly sales target treadmill and if something won't deliver immediate results, it gets kicked down the road.

2. The sales-led culture.

As a result of point one, the net result is that marketing gets relegated to a support function for sales. Again, all focus goes to short-term tactical lead generation activities at the expense of brand building.

3. The product-led growth culture.

Don't get me wrong, I'm a big fan of PLG and creating a product that has a fantastic user-journey at the heart of it is a great thing. But what some product-led businesses forget is that people don't make decisions to buy just based on product features alone. Decision-making is not driven by rationality alone.

4. **The misunderstanding of 'brand'.**

This is the biggie. Brand building requires long-term thinking and investment. As we'll explore in this book, it's criminally under-invested within B2B businesses.

Fundamentally, we need to flip our thinking from seeing B2B buyers as anything different to B2C buyers. We are selling to people, those squishy human-like things that sit in chairs and make decisions based on subjectivity and irrational biases.

We often overcomplicate the process of marketing. Irrespective of channel, platform or medium - as businesses we are **simply seeking to build trust.**

Trust is at the core of all buying decisions and how do we typically refer to a business that is trusted by many? That's right. We call it 'A brand'.

Trust grows through word of mouth and the channel that spreads word of mouth like no other is social media.

As a result, 'branding' in B2B and how our stories are shared on social media channels has never been more essential to unlock growth in this rapidly changing environment.

In this book, we'll explore how B2B's can power growth through social media, exploring buyer psychology, storytelling, creativity, community and emerging trends and technology, providing you with a framework to unlock this burgeoning opportunity.

B2B's are behind the social media curve. It's time to rethink our strategies, take action and change the status quo.

If you are a leader of a B2B Software-as-a-Service business that wants to create a long-term growth advantage or a marketer in B2B SaaS that wants to drive culture change in how your business approaches social media, this book is for you.

Introducing the '6 C's' and the SOCIAL 3.0 framework

The aim of this book is to both help you understand the opportunity at hand and help you create a strategy to harness it. To breakdown the areas we need to consider as part of our plan of action we have split this book into 6 areas. We call them the '6 C's'

- Customer
- Context
- Creativity
- Community
- Channels
- Calculation

Each of these areas forms part of the SOCIAL 3.0 framework which sets the scene for the book, helping you work through each step in turn, leave you with a full, 360 view of how to harness this opportunity.

The framework

1. Creating a growth model. Introducing the SOCIAL 3.0 framework
2. The power of a brand. Understanding the importance of brand building for B2B.
3. We're all human. Understanding buyer psychology.
4. First principles. The six fundamentals of social media marketing

Customer

5. Creating your audience. How to rethink market orientation.
6. Creating your value proposition. How to use data to craft the right message
7. Customer Discovery. How to ensure your message resonates

Context

8. Telling stories. Using storytelling to unlock creativity.
9. Objective Setting. How to set meaningful social media goals.

Creativity

10. Qualitative Creativity. Creating content 'Pillars'.

11. Quantitative Creativity. Harnessing data-led insight from our content, our competitors and the broader market.

12. Inspired Creativity. Taking advantage of trends and empowering organisation-wide creativity.

Community

13. Building trust. The importance of employee advocacy.

14. Creators and Influencers. Building trust through affiliation.

15. The power of Community. Creating trust through connection.

Channels

16. Owned Channels. Core, emerging and the impact of Web3 and Metaverse.

17. Earned and Paid Channels. Maximising growth from advocacy and paid media

Calculation

18. Evaluating and tracking success

CHAPTER 1
THE SOCIAL 3.0 FRAMEWORK

From my experience, B2B's typically fall into one of two camps.

1. They are sales-led.

This has typically been the orientation of many enterprise focussed B2B businesses. Sales teams are a key element of growth for many businesses and have the ability to build relationships and trust at a personal level. But the challenge that comes with this culture is a fixation on short term results.

For these types of organisations, marketing is typically seen as a sales support function and very little investment goes into the long term view of both brand and product development.

2. They are product-led.

Product led growth (PLG) has become a popular term in SaaS and relates to engineering the product to be a growth engine for the business, encouraging quick adoption, a fast time to the 'wow' moment and a strong viral coefficient. All of this is good stuff, but an engineering-led culture that is driven by data can over-index on rationality, missing the most important reasons people make decisions, which is always based on emotion.

As with most things in life, the right answer is a balance between the two approaches. In all cases, I think we can agree that everything begins and ends with our customer. And let's be honest, in the eyes of the customer, **the best product is the one they know.**

This type of approach is known as 'market' orientation.

Market orientation is a business philosophy where the focus is on identifying customer needs or wants and meeting them. This is opposed to product orientation – where the focus is on establishing selling points for existing goods.

Marketing Strategist and Keynote Speaker True Tamplin said this about market orientation: "Market orientation is absolutely essential in today's saturated world. Focusing on the customers' needs and creating organic brand loyalty is the foundation for lasting, consistent growth."

This market orientated approach is endorsed by marketing superstar, Mark Ritson. He has long campaigned for marketers to think of the process of marketing as; Diagnosis, Strategy and Tactics. In that order.

The graphic below encapsulates this perfectly. Many businesses consider the product before they truly understand the needs of the buyer and many marketers often skip to the fun bit; 'promotion' — which is often the case in sales-led cultures.

Marketing, Product and Sales all have the same ambition: to meet the needs of the customers, to delight them and to keep them coming back.

We need a new model to align everyone's objectives and unlock growth in a market-oriented way, that's underpinned by 'Diagnosis, Strategy and Tactics'. This approach will not only supercharge your social media efforts, but will shape your broader content and marketing strategy.

This approach calls for a new framework, we call it SOCIAL 3.0.

Introducing the SOCIAL 3.0 Framework

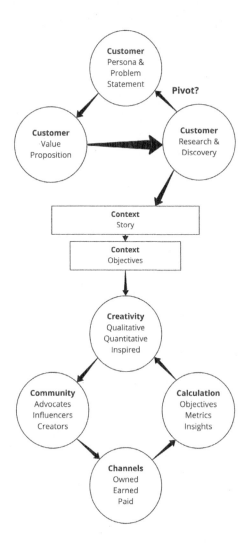

Customer

Step 1. Persona & Problem Statement

As any market-oriented approach should do, we begin with the customer.

Objective: To understand who you are trying to serve and the change you seek to make.

Action: Document your target persona and focus on psychographics over demographics. Document the challenges you believe this audience faces and what their alternative solutions are.

Outcome: Establish a 'Minimum Viable Audience'

Step 2. Value Proposition

Objective: Based on your assumptions from step 1, we need to align who we are trying to serve with the change we seek to make in order to craft a value proposition.

Action: Think of your value proposition in three ways; *why* (your purpose and mission), *how* (how your solution addresses the problem statement) *and what* (what your solution is)

Outcome: Establish a hypothesis of your value proposition

Step 3. Customer Discovery

Objective: Augment your value proposition with objective market research data and test your messaging with prospective and current customers

Action: Use market research tools to gain objective data to help inform your value proposition. Organise time with prospective and current customers to understand if the messaging resonates.

Outcome: If your value proposition resonates with the audience, use the additional insights from these users to further hone your messaging into a user story. If your value proposition falls short, return to step 1 and revisit the persona and problem statement.

Context

Step 4. Story

As in the popular board game Monopoly, unless you get the story right through interactions with real people in the 'Customer discovery' phase, you cannot pass 'Go'.

Your story predicates everything you'll do from here on in, so it's essential we get this right.

Step 5. Objectives

Before we go into creation mode, we need to get clear on our objectives. Remember, the SOCIAL 3.0 Framework is about focussing on a key audience segment (known as your Minimum Viable Audience) and in time, we might well construct several of these for different audience types, so it's likely objectives will differ depending on the audience.

But for now, before we progress to the 'Creativity' step, we should have the right story to tell and be clear about what we are trying to achieve.

Creativity

Step 6. Quantitative, Qualitative and Inspired Creativity

Objective: To foster creativity through research and inspiration

Action: Use your qualitative and quantitative learnings in the 'Customer Discovery' step, along with inspiration gained from competitors and trends to establish initial content ideas

Outcome: To create content 'themes' for your strategy and create a process that facilitates continual inspiration.

Community

Step 7. Advocates, Influencers and Creators

Objective: To find others you can collaborate with to fuel your growth.

Action: Look both internally within your business and externally to create a list of individuals that would contribute to your growth. Understand the value exchange with these individuals that ensures all collaborations are mutually beneficial.

Outcome: Build relationships with creators, influencers and advocates you can work with both internally and externally

Channels

Step 8. Owned, Earned and Paid Channels

Objective: To understand the channels that will drive both short and long term impact.

Action: Research the channels that will help support your objectives. Establish a balanced mix between paid content (ads and influencer partnerships), owned (content you create for your own channels) and earned (PR, word of mouth and advocacy)

Outcome: Create a plan that ensures campaigns are equally supported across multiple channels.

Calculation

Step 9. Objectives, Metrics and Insights

Objective: To understand the 'metrics that matter' and create a reporting methodology that allows you to simply track the progress of your strategy,

Action: Discover the metrics that best underpin your chosen objective. For example, the metrics could be 'share of voice' or 'impressions' if our objective is to grow brand awareness.

Outcome: Create a reporting process that enables you to simply track progress and learn for future iterations. The learnings from our analysis will inform the quantitive analysis element of step 6.

We're now going to dive into each of these steps, from Customer to Calculation over the remaining 15 chapters.

CHAPTER 2
THE POWER OF A BRAND

People buy with emotion and justify with logic.

In our personal lives, I think we can all agree with this. But for some reason, the moment we start talking about our product or business, we completely lose sight of this.

Just take a casual look through some B2B 'brands' social feeds and homepages — how much messaging is rational vs. emotional? Exactly.

No one falls in love with logic.

This is why 'brand-building' (the process of creating an emotional connection between you and your audience) is so important. Your 'brand' is your unfair advantage that weighs a buyer's decision in your favour.

Our B2C marketer friends get this. A Rolex or Casio watch both tell the time adequately well, but their brands mean VERY different things to their respective buyers.

But why is that?

In general, there are three things that cause people to make decisions

- Status - How will I be perceived by others and does this move me up or down relative to the social hierarchy?

- Affiliation - What connections will this bring and to what extent does being affiliated with something change how I see myself and how I'm seen by others?

- Convenience - Will this make my life easier?

Ultimately, a brand sells time, feelings, status, and connection, not functional benefits.
For example,

Rolex sell social status, not watches
Supreme sells scarcity, not clothing
Harley-Davidson sells a lifestyle, not motorbikes
Apple sells affiliation, not electronics

So, it's clear that people don't want what you make. They want the way it will make them feel.

We'll explore buyer psychology more in the next chapter.

B2C's understand the human emotions that are at the core of purchasing decisions, and this is why I'm still deeply saddened when I see B2B's over-indexing on short-term promotional activity at the expense of building a brand that truly means something in the customers' mind.

Omobono put the percentage of budget B2B's put towards brand building as part of the marketing budget at just 17%.

I do get it though, B2B's are on the monthly/quarterly results treadmill, often fuelled by investor pressure. In this desire for short-term performance improvement, strategic thinking get replaced with tactical comments like; 'If we could get 100 more leads, we'd be hitting the target'.

This then results in more efforts (and budget) being directed towards short-term performance marketing, relegating the marketing function to a sales-support function. As a result, the brand gets under-invested in, overall growth from word of mouth and general awareness gets slower and thus, the cycle continues.

To borrow from Professor Mark Ritson; 'marketers are so busy picking the low hanging fruit, they are forgetting to water the tree.'

This thinking is not new. The IPA's book, The Long and the Short of it, looked at 996 award-winning campaigns featuring 700 brands across 83 categories, to determine the factors which contributed to both short and long-term business growth.

They found that whilst promotional activity drives effectiveness over the short term (more sales), it is brand building campaigns that create large meaningful impact over the long term (profit gains, market share, unprompted awareness, etc).

IPA's book clearly outlines a model for how businesses should balance both short and long-term targets; 60% of the budget should go on brand building, with 40% on short-term sales conversion activity. Way off where B2B's are today.

As B2B marketers, we typically think that brand-building is for consumer-orientated brands, falling into the trap of thinking that business-orientated purchases are purely rational decisions.

But this is very much not the case and here's four reasons why.

1. B2B products are often hard to buy and complex to understand.

B2B purchases often come with a lot of factors to consider. In 'high consideration' decisions like this, a strong brand simplifies decision making.

As Daniel Kahnemann argues in Thinking Fast and Slow, when we have a difficult decision to make, we often replace it with a simpler one. When faced with weighing up a set of complex options, it's much easier to replace this decision with a simpler question; 'which one of these brands am I familiar with'. This is what marketers describe as 'mental availability'.

The incredible thing is that we are almost totally unaware of doing this. As the psychologist Jonathon Haidt describes: "We like to think of our conscious mind as the

President in the White House, dishing out orders. But in reality, it functions like a press secretary, automatically justifying any position we take."

Again, back to the earlier point; We make decisions with emotions and justify with logic.

2. Brands are a common language

B2B purchases are further complicated by the fact that usually multiple stakeholders are involved in the purchase, often with competing agendas and requirements.

Strong brands cut across these differing agendas. Whilst the functional requirements might be different for each stakeholder — your brand is the story that unites everyone.

For example, we might not agree on what's most important, but we can all agree that Microsoft is better known, and thus seen as more reputable, than an unknown start-up tech company.

3. Strong brands minimise the risk of getting blamed if things go wrong.

Rory Sutherland amusingly points out that: "The key driver in B2C purchases is maximising pleasure, whereas the key driver in B2B purchases is avoiding blame."

You might remember the old adage: 'No one gets fired for buying IBM'. Strong brands give B2B purchasers the confidence that if the purchase is a huge disaster, they have something to hide behind. 'Who would have thought this strong brand was so poor? Their reputation more than justified the decision, etc.'

Simply put, as humans we 'satisfice,' choosing the least uncertain option, not the best option. In 1956, a genius named Herbert Simon introduced the satisficing concept, which won him a Noble Prize in Economics. 'Satisficing' is a portmanteau of 'sufficing' and 'satisfying', and it's a foundational concept in behavioural economics and cognitive psychology.

Really a brand is just a tool for humans to 'satisfice.' Buyers don't want the best possible product, buyers want good-enough products that come to mind easily (mental availability) and are easy to purchase (physical availability).

Recent research from the Ehrenberg-Bass Institute[1] found that, even in high-involvement purchases, very little evaluation occurs. For instance, when B2B buyers need a new financial service, 47% go straight to their existing bank, and 75% of those who claim to shop around also end up with their existing bank. And most buyers don't even consider more than two brands.

4. Strong brands add a premium to otherwise often commoditised products.

Many B2B brands sell commoditised products or services, with very little differentiation between themselves and their competition. This is not an issue in itself, but without a strong brand, B2B's end up competing on price with heavy discounting. Strong brands are differentiated in the minds of buyers, holding a price premium, and helping to encourage customers to buy more, and buy more often.

These points are further demonstrated by Les Binet and Peter Fields' excellent study on the 5 principles of B2B growth. The research identified a clear tendency for customers that are 'out of market' to be emotionally led.

---

[1] https://www.marketingweek.com/ehrenberg-bass-linkedin-b2b-buyers/

'Out of market' refers to when a customer is not actively looking to purchase your product. This is particularly important, because it's estimated that only 5% of a total audience are 'in market' at any one time[2] so if we want to appeal to the other 95%, we need to be emotionally led.

For in-market customers, **be rational.**

For out-of-market customers, **be emotional.**

Source: IPA Databank, 1998-2018 B2B Cases

As an example, cloud storage is about as commoditised as you can get, but Dropbox have built a fantastic business engineered around word of mouth growth through a brilliant user experience.

This is a long-term brand strategy in full force.

---

[2] https://www.marketingweek.com/ehrenberg-bass-linkedin-b2b-buyers/

The challenge now is to align what you say with what you do. Your behaviour, as a brand, goes beyond features, price, customer support... It's everything that you do (and also everything you don't.)

So, we now understand the importance of brand-building, the power of emotion in decision making and how we need to adjust our budgets to focus on the long term. Let's now look deeper into the elements of human psychology that drive buying behaviour.

CHAPTER 3
WE'RE ALL HUMAN.
UNDERSTANDING BUYER
PSYCHOLOGY

In Joseph Pine's TED Talk, 'What consumers want',[3] he suggests that in the evolution from the agricultural to the industrial and now the information revolution, what we want from the products we buy has evolved.

---

[3] https://www.ted.com/talks/joseph_pine_what_consumers_want?language=en

In the Agricultural age, it was all about 'commodities' — the essentials we needed to survive. As cultures evolved into the industrial age, the focus switched to 'goods' and the continual lowering of costs through increasingly efficient manufacturing processes. Most recently, in the information age, many nations have developed into 'service' economies.

However, as markets expand and products proliferate, consumers are increasingly drawn to customised and personal experiences.

This desire for the customisation of products has led brands to strive to create more unique and authentic services for customers. A prime example of this is Airbnb. This multi-billion dollar business is built on the customers' desire for unique and authentic experiences. The key here is in the word 'authenticity'. Authenticity is a key component of influence (we'll cover 7 more later on) and, according to Joseph Pine, authenticity is at the core of a buyer's innate desire to connect with experiences at an emotional level.

For businesses, authenticity is about being true to themselves and reflecting that in the words they say and in the way they act. In other words, it's about businesses living their values.

To bring this to life for your business, provide a place for consumers to experience who you are. This spans from the events you run, to the communities you create, to the employees whom you want to highlight publicly to the charity endeavours you are engaged with. Essentially provide prospects and customers with an opportunity to connect with your business at a human level.

In the aforementioned TED talk, Joseph also lays out a simple way of understanding what drives customers' purchasing behaviour in different product categories.

Product Type	Business Value I	Consumer Drive
Commodities	Supply	Availability
Goods	Control	Cost
Services	Improve	Quality
Experiences	Render	Authenticity

As we mentioned a moment ago, as goods, products and services have evolved, the way that businesses were required to compete have changed to match the evolving needs of the consumer.

We've gone from commodities where a business would compete to have the best supply to match the consumer need for availability (take petrol as a good example of this) to where businesses need to 'render' or wrap a personalised, human experience to match the consumer desire for authenticity.

To explore the concept of authenticity in marketing in a little more depth, let's look at the 'Pratfall effect'.

This idea was first discussed by Elliot Aronson, Professor of Psychology at Harvard in the 1960s: The premise is that if you admit a weakness and exhibit flaws, you become more appealing.

Aronson recruited someone to take part in a quiz in which the participant does incredibly well. After he's done however, he makes what Americans would call a 'pratfall' or a small blunder, in other words. He stands up and he spills a cup of coffee down himself.

Aronson takes that recording and he plays it to participants in his experiment in one of two ways:

1) They hear the entire episode or,
2) They just hear the great quiz performance.

And then Aronson asks everyone, 'how appealing do you find this guy?' The people who've heard the mistake found the contestant to be significantly more appealing. [4]

As humans, we don't trust perfection, yet as brands we constantly strive for it. Here's another good example;

In 2015, Northwestern University scraped 111,000 product reviews across 22 product categories and analysed the correlation between the average review rating and the likelihood to purchase.

Here's what they've found: The likelihood to purchase increased as the average review rating went up until it reached a tipping point, somewhere between 4.2 and 4.4 out of 5. After that point, the likelihood to purchase decreased as the average rating went up.

---

[4] https://www.everyonehatesmarketers.com/articles/pratfall-effect-marketing

Being 'real' and showing imperfection is a leap for brands, but it's appealing when brands have the courage to show it. Oatly is one of the few companies that truly understand the power of authenticity...

"This tastes like sh*t! Blah!"

That's a real comment from a real person who tried one of our oatmilks for the first time. Some people just don't like it. They think it tastes like oats, because it does taste like oats. Here's the good part. If you don't like the taste of our oatmilks, you don't have to drink them. Taste is personal which is why we don't take it personal if you don't like how they taste.

There is, however, a growing number of people who find oatmilk delicious. Who can taste the balance of protein, fiber, unsaturated fats and carbs and know that it makes them feel good. So, give it a go and if you don't like it you can always give it to someone you don't like. That's what business students call a win-win.

THE ORIGINAL

OAT-LY!

OAT-MILK

No dairy. No nuts. No gluten.

100% Vegan

64 fl oz (1/2 GAL) (1.89 L)

Authenticity is just one element of understanding buyer psychology, let's now dive into the nascent field of 'Neuromarketing' — the study of human emotion in decision making.

To give an example of the power of understanding, or in this case, misunderstanding the power of emotion in decision making, let's look at one of the most famous corporate failings in the recent history of business. I am, of course, talking about the fabled introduction of 'New Coke'.

Despite Coca-Cola bringing the world's best-selling soft drink, during the 70's and 80's, rival Pepsi continued to gain market share, due to its aggressive "Pepsi Challenge" campaign in which consumers taking blind taste tests were surprised to learn they preferred the flavour of Pepsi. To the shock of Coca-Cola, internal taste tests yielded the same results.

Company executives grew to become convinced that Pepsi's taste was the reason for Coca-Cola's declining market share.

On April 23, 1985, excited Coca-Cola executives proudly introduced the Coke's new formula to the world, called

'New Coke'. They also retired the old formula at the same time.

This was a particularly bold move.

That said, they had hardly made a rash decision unsupported by data. After all, they had performed 190,000 blind taste tests on U.S. and Canadian consumers.

But why was it then, just weeks after launch, were Coca-Cola getting 8,000 disgruntled consumer calls per day and seeing protests of 'old' Coke drinkers across the country?

The problem is that the company had underestimated drinkers' emotional attachments to the brand. Never did its market research testers ask subjects how they would feel if the new formula replaced the old one.

79 days after the introduction of New Coke, Classic Coke was reintroduced. Coca-Cola president Donald Keough admitted after the fact; "The simple fact is that all the time and money and skill poured into consumer research on the new Coca-Cola, it could not measure or reveal the deep and abiding emotional attachment to original Coca-Cola felt by so many people,"

Simply put, the Coca-Cola team failed to understand the impact of emotions in decision making.

Further studies have been subsequently carried out on this phenomena. Dr. Terry Wu goes into detail in this excellent TED talk [5] citing a recent example which supported Coca-Cola's study that many still prefer the taste of Pepsi to Coke in blind taste tests, but when the taste tests are no longer blind, consumers will most often choose Coke over Pepsi.

The reason this happens is rooted in biology, not just psychology. Our brains 'Limbic system' is the part of our brain that governs both emotion and behaviour and is actively engaged when we are in the process of decision making. This is why it is difficult to remove emotions from our decisions and make a decision based on rationality alone.

This is also why Dr. Wu's TED talk is so interesting, his field, 'neuromarketing' explores the science behind consumer decisions. It's such an important element to understand in marketing as its thought that 95% of our decisions are made subconsciously.

---

[5] https://www.youtube.com/watch?v=UEtE-el6KKs

Basically, we, as humans, cannot make decisions without emotions

Coke is a brilliant example of this. Coca-Cola are masters of advertising and have produced advertising campaigns that have become ingrained in modern culture.

From the 'holidays are coming' Christmas ad, to the 'share a Coke' campaign which involved personalised bottles, to the distinctive 'pop' and 'tsssssh' of opening a bottle of Coke. Like it or not, Coca-Cola has become associated with friends, family and good times. That's an incredibly powerful emotion to conjure and that, right there, is at the very heart of what a 'brand' is — the emotional connection between product and consumer.

This leads us right back to neuromarketing and our limbic system.

It's estimated that adults make 35,000 decisions per day [6] — that's rather a lot, so our brains have evolved to prevent us from getting overwhelmed with the sheer number of choices we need to make in a day. It does this by

---

6 https://www.inc.com/heidi-zak/adults-make-more-than-35000-decisions-per-day-here-are-4-ways-to-prevent-mental-burnout.html

shortcutting our decision-making by defaulting to previous patterns and feelings.

So, if we made a decision on a certain basis before, we're likely to be consistent with that if we are faced with a similar decision. Also, if we made a decision that we associate with a positive emotional outcome, we are likely to make the same decision again. It's this point that's at the core of Coke's brand and the reason why New Coke failed so dramatically.

It's clear that our limbic system plays a key role in decision making, so let's now look at that in some more detail.

In one of the most popular TED talks of all time, 'How great leaders inspire action',[7] Simon Sinek outlines one of the most important (and my personal favourite) communication concepts.

Known as the 'Golden Circle', this framework is built on the basis that *people don't buy* **what** *you do, they buy* **why** *you do it.*

---

[7] https://www.ted.com/talks/simon_sinek_how_great_leaders_inspire_action?language=en

Simon Sinek's premise is that businesses communicate in the wrong order, starting with *what* they do and *how* they do it, but missing the key element of *why* they do it. It's the way we've always been taught to sell and market products; Feature, Advantage and Benefit, in that order.

Take this ContentCal example; *'At ContentCal, we provide social media management tools for small businesses. We do this by providing a simple and intuitive calendar layout, to help you grow your social media following'*.

Not awful, right? But is it any different to what others would say? Probably not. Does it conjure an emotional connection? Definitely not.

The 'Golden Circle' sets about reversing this concept, communicating from the inside out, quite literally, starting with *why* you do something, *how* you do it and closing with *what* you do.

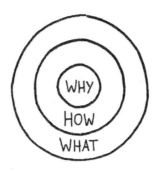

Let's try this description again, but this time using the principles of the 'Golden Circle'...

'We believe in the power of connection. Connections create communities, and strong communities create unstoppable businesses. We do this by helping you build communities around your business through simple, yet powerful social media tools.'

It begins with a clear purpose (the 'why) that speaks at an emotional level. The *how* allows you to be more descriptive in how you seek to address the 'why' and the *what* is the last important element and will leave the smallest impression on the target audience, but clearly, you still need to say what it is that you do, but importantly, it needs to be in the context of your *why*.

Simply put, it's about winning hearts first. Once we've won hearts, the minds of our audience will surely follow.

This 'Golden Circle' concept might seem like a phycological framework, but again, it's rooted in biology, not psychology.

If you take a look at a cross-section of the human brain, you'll see alignment with the 'Golden Circle' concept. [8]

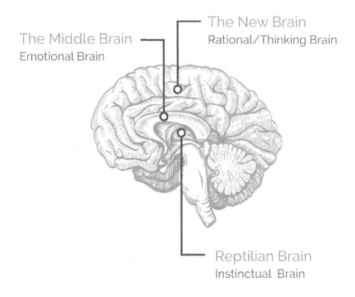

The Middle Brain
Emotional Brain

The New Brain
Rational/Thinking Brain

Reptilian Brain
Instinctual Brain

We are quite literally communicating from the inside out. Information is processed in the Limbic system (The Middle Brain) know as the 'emotional brain' first, after which the Neo-cortex 'the rational brain' gets to work.

8 https://hellonextstep.com/resource-detail-are-you-marketing-to-all-3-parts-of-your-users-brain.html

The Limbic system works much quicker than the Neocortex and as a result, draws conclusions before we've had a chance to rationalise them. If we think of people being 'hot-headed' or putting 'heart before head' or maybe those that made a decision because they 'felt it in their gut' — none of this has anything to do with hearts or guts controlling our thoughts, it's all happening in our Limbic system.

Think of the Limbic system as the gatekeeper to the Neocortex. If we want to convince someone of our argument with data, we need to win over their emotional brain first. This is why data is useless without a story — something we'll cover later in this book.

We're starting to see that humans are essentially irrational creatures, but that there are some universal laws that we can apply that are based not just on psychological principles, but on biological facts.

But, before we start applying these learnings into how we communicate with our target audience, we need to dig deeper into the factors that influence buyer behaviour, which will inform how we communicate and share our stories.

In Dr. Robert Cialdini's research-led book; 'Influence; The power of persuasion' he identified seven universal shortcuts that guide human behaviour, they are: Reciprocity. Consistency. Consensus. Likeability. Authority. Scarcity and Unity. [9]

All of these point to a clear science of how we are persuaded and how these factors influence our emotional reactions.

Reciprocity.

Reciprocity calls on the strong social contract we enter into when someone shows us unsolicited good will. Simply put, we are more likely to respond in kind if we have received something first. In Dr. Cialdini's study, they looked at the value of tips given in a restaurant.

When a server gives the diner a single mint along with their bill, tips increased by 3%. Interestingly, if the mints are doubled, tips don't double — they quadruple to a 14% increase in tips. But, most interestingly of all, if a waiter provides one mint, starts to walk away from the table, then

---

[9] https://www.amazon.co.uk/Influence-Psychology-Robert-Cialdini-PhD/dp/006124189X

turns back and says; *'for you nice people, here's an extra mint'*, tips go through the roof, a 23% increase.

It's not about *what* gift was given, but *how* it was given. The key here is to be both personalised and unexpected in your gift. This approach creates a strong social contract and dramatically increases your chance of your request being accepted.

Scarcity.

Simply put, people want more of what they can't have.

Wordle is a perfect recent example of this, as shared in Richard Shotten and Will Hanmer-Lloyds' excellent Marketing Week blog.;[10]

Wordle is a simple word game in which you have six attempts to guess a five-letter word. It hasn't always been so successful. The prototype, created by British software engineer Josh Wardle, was launched among his friends in 2013. However, they were so apathetic he scrapped the project.

---

[10] https://www.marketingweek.com/richard-shotton-scarcity-wordle/

A few years later, Wardle became hooked on the New York Times cryptic crossword. He wondered if his fascination was due to the fact that only one puzzle a day was released. He was always left wanting more.

Taking the crossword as inspiration, Wardle rejigged the prototype: now players were limited to a single puzzle a day. According to Wardle, he wanted the game to be like a croissant, a delightful snack that is sampled occasionally.

It was a small but powerful tweak. The game now has more than 300,000 daily users and Wardle attributes the success to that simple restriction.

Could this simple tweak really be the difference between worldwide hit and obsolescence?

Studies in behavioural science seem to suggest so.

The most famous experiment in this area was conducted by Stephen Worchel. In 1975 he recruited 134 undergraduates and asked them to rate the quality of a batch of cookies. The participants tasted the cookies from a glass jar containing either 2 or 10 biscuits.

When the cookies were in scarce supply, they were rated as significantly more attractive and likeable. Furthermore, participants were willing to pay 25% more for them.

Scarcity is a regular launch feature for tech products: Clubhouse is a perfect example of this. It's the very definition of internet hype, and at its peak, people were even selling their invites to others that were desperate to join.

People desperately wanted to be part of the club, even though they had no idea what was happening on the platform. Again, this desire was not based on rationality. [11]

To further evidence this lack of rationality and the power of scarcity, just a few months after users were selling invites to Clubhouse and media hype was at its peak, Clubhouse decided to open up the platform for all and this act was like letting the air out of a balloon. Clubhouse is now struggling for growth and in less than a year of it being lauded as the next great revolution of social media, there's now an avalanche of articles questioning whether Clubhouse's relevance has already peaked. [12]

---

[11] https://www.newsweek.com/clubhouse-ebay-listings-sell-invites-audio-app-ios-hundreds-dollars-1571609)

[12] https://onezero.medium.com/what-happened-to-clubhouse-b347fed28b77

Clubhouse's story is akin to Wordle's but in reverse and it clearly demonstrates the emotional power of scarcity.

The fear of loss, or the more recently popularised FOMO (Fear of missing out), might seem like a trivialised meme, but it's at the core of our psychology and the emotional distress we feel from the fear of losing or missing something is far stronger than the emotions we feel when we gain.

The mix of psychological experiments and practical examples should give you the inspiration to evaluate the effects of scarcity on your brand.

That might mean offering limited access to new releases, or access to a private membership community or discounts for customers that meet a certain criteria — there are many ways to leverage the emotional power of scarcity.

To use Josh Wardle's wonderful turn of phrase, take inspiration from the croissant. Sometimes it's better to be an occasional treat that leaves people wanting more.

The next concept to explore is the power of Authority.

Authority

In general, people are more likely to react favourably to a person in a position of authority.

In one of Dr. Cialdini's studies, drivers were less likely to honk their horn at the drivers of expensive executive cars as opposed to drivers of less expensive vehicles following an incident. In another experiment, physicians were more likely to have patients accept their recommended course of treatment after their medical qualifications were clearly displayed. In addition, one real estate agency was able to increase the volume of property appraisals by 20% and the number of signed contracts by 15% by arranging for the reception staff who answered customer enquiries to first mention their colleagues credentials and expertise before putting the call through.

What's interesting about authority, is that it seems to make no difference in its influential power as to the justification of this authority. As we saw in the real estate example, authority was implied through an introduction and if we think about this for our businesses, we'll want to consider reviews, award wins and customer testimonials as a way to take advantage of the influential power of authority.

Authority also plays a key part in some practical examples we'll provide later in the book, particularly around employee advocacy and influencer marketing.

Consistency.

People like to be consistent with decisions they have previously made. We touched on this earlier in the way that our brains shortcut decision making to default to previous patterns.

People will be more likely to accept your request if they have said yes to smaller requests previously. In one famous study, homeowners were unsurprisingly unwilling to erect a 'please drive slowly' wooden board on their front lawns as a part of a driving safety campaign. In a similar neighbourhood, homeowners were 4 times more likely to accept the request. Why? Because ten days previously, the homeowners had agreed to put a postcard in their front window displaying the same message.

To apply this logic to B2B software, we need to look for smaller commitments that will increase the likelihood of our future, larger requests being accepted. This could be free trials (a very popular method of software growth), but rather than just the usage of a trial being the opportunity to encourage the persuasive power of consistency, the key is to encourage the user to create something, or do something in your product that relates to the biggest request you'll be asking for. (Usually asking the user to change their behaviour to use your tool or product).

Behaviour change is challenging but incredibly powerful. Once someone has begun to work a different way, they are likely to become consistent with that change in future, making it easier to persuade with a larger commitment.

The 5th principle is liking.

Liking.

We are drawn to those that we like. 'Liking' can be broken down into 4 areas:

1. We are drawn to those that are like us.
2. We like those that pay us compliments
3. We like those that corporate with us
4. We like those that like us

In a series of negotiation studies carried out in 2 well-known business schools, one group was told to get straight to the point. This group saw a 55% success rate in negotiations. A separate group was told to exchange personal information and share something they had in common and then told to begin negotiating. The success rate of negotiations went up to 90%.

To explore the principle of liking further, *Likeonomics* author, Rohit Bhargava breaks down the concept of 'liking' into 5-steps:

- **Truth** - We are drawn to those that inspire trust. For businesses that can mean inconvenient truths, or taking ownership if something goes wrong.

- **Relevance** - To truly understand your audience you need to speak their language. Liking happens when people feel both seen and heard

- **Unselfishness** - Businesses need to consider their broader impact on both society and the environment. This goes beyond hollow CSR goals, and is becoming increasingly important for the modern buyer.

- **Simplicity** - As we've already touched on, our brain's default to simple choices. Maximising simplicity is essential for liking

- **Timing** - This is about maximising convenience and delivering solutions when customers need it most.

But, if you wanted to cut right to the core of liking and sum it up in one word, it is 'trust'. Trust is the foundation of liking, and conveniently enough is exactly the acronym that the above points spell out.

To apply the principle of liking to your business, it's essential to humanise your brand by highlighting and promoting employees publicly. Give your employees a voice to share their experiences publicly. This will allow for your prospects to identify with the personalities behind the brand, helping form a more personal, emotional and trusting bond with your brand.

In addition, pay compliments to your target audience, even if it's through your messaging. For example; '*We see you social media marketers, you do an incredible job despite being underpaid and under-appreciated*'. This immediately helps you create 'relevance' with our target audience as we are naturally drawn to people who are like us.

Consensus.

Consensus is one of the primary decision-making tools for buyers. Consensus allows us to shortcut decision-making by looking to the actions of others to influence our decision.

We might also call it social-proof, but it's why word-of-mouth is still the most powerful marketing channel. Social proof helps us 'satisfice' — enabling us to settle for the most convenient option that ultimately feels the least risky option. (In B2B, buyers are even more motivated by loss aversion). Being recommended a product or service by someone you trust is the ultimate shortcut for buyers looking to simplify their decision making.

To apply this principle, ask for reviews from customers, ensure your TrustPilot (or similar) rankings are strong and point to that in your marketing content. Use phases like; *'2,000 customers have rated us 4.7 * for transforming for their content marketing results'*.

Also, consider the impact of User Generated Content (UGC) in highlighting and championing your customers' use of your product to encourage consensus. We'll touch on UGC later on in the book, but it's said that UGC impacts 79% of purchasing decisions and 84% of consumers say they trust peer recommendations above all other sources of advertising.[13]

Achieving consensus decisions can also be driven through community orientated activity. Creating a community of like minded individuals with a common purpose enjoyed by both customers and prospects is a fantastic way to use the power of consensus to weigh decision making in your favour.

Community takes us nicely onto the final power of persuasion.

Unity.

Communities have become increasingly recognised as an incredibly powerful marketing tool. So much so, we've begun to see the dawn of the term 'Community Led Growth'.

Let's explore Community Led Growth in a little more depth.

---

[13] https://everyonesocial.com/blog/user-generated-content-statistics/)

Historically there have been two ways of scaling a SaaS business. One is 'top-down', think about the Oracle or SAP's of the world, where a solution is sold to an executive team that mandates the changes across the business. The second model is 'bottom-up', a good example of which is Slack or Box. In this model products are used (usually initially on a free basis) by the employees within a business, departments began to subscribe as they see increasing value in the product and eventually the virality of the product spreads its usage across the enterprise.

There is now the dawn of a third dimension - Community Led Growth.

What's changed is that people have more agency than they ever have to decide what tools they use at work. The days of mandating an organisation-wide change from the top down appear to be coming to an end — especially as hybrid working becomes the norm.

We know the power 'consensus' has to influence others — people typically seek the insights from others as to the best products and services to use. This is happening through social media influencers, on review sites, in Reddit threads, through user generated content on TikTok and in

Facebook Groups. The surround sound of social media allows individuals to understand what they need to know about any given product.

So what do you do to harness this as a business? You turn to the world around you and you find other people to tell your story.

A perfect real-life example of this is B2B organisation software, Notion. Notion has nurtured a loyal community of creators and fans to fuel growth, propelling the business to a $10 billion valuation.

Camille Ricketts was employee number one in marketing at Notion. Camille saw that there were a couple of people on Twitter who were very, very vocal about how wonderful Notion was. She saw this and she realised, "Okay, this is our community. What do we need to do to embrace these people and bring them in?".

At the same time, there was a Notion fan site generating 80,000 hits per month run by Ben Lang. Camille had the foresight to hire Ben to run the Notion community and use this site as the foundation for the community. Camille and Ben then decided to connect all of the Notion ambassadors and realised there was a simple way to make these people feel connected to both each other and to Notion as a business.

The Notion team began running community events, allowing users to come and ask questions and make recommendations for the development of the product. In return, the community got early access to new features and were truly listened to as they became a kind of 'customer advisory board'. Making these community members feel listened to inspires trust and helps community members feel like Notion truly has the best interests of the community at heart.

Skip forward to today, Notion has over 200 ambassadors in over 23 countries, the community team all know them personally, understanding their passions and deeply understanding what they're there for and why they're on this journey with Notion.

What truly unlocks Community-Led Growth for Notion is that the people leading the company are right at the forefront of it all. Today there are about 145,000 in Notion's Subreddit, multiple Facebook Groups (one in Korea alone has 34,000 members).

There is a real sense of belonging and unity in the Notion community and the benefits of the community span all elements of the business, from generating awareness, to education, to product development, to referrals and word of mouth and customer support.

In the words of Notion CRO, Olivia Nottebohm;

"You need community to win. Be grateful to the community. It's really amazing when people spend the time to get deep into the product, to fall in love with the product and then decide to turn out to the world and tell your story for you." [14]

Notion's focus on community is not rocket-science, but it's the gap that separates great companies from the rest.

Before we get into the '6C's of the SOCIAL 3.0 framework, there's one further concept we want to explore, which will help us ensure we make the best possible decisions with our social media strategy.

---

[14] https://www.saastr.com/how-community-led-growth-drives-product-led-growth/

CHAPTER 4
FIRST-PRINCIPLES. THE SIX FUNDAMENTALS OF SOCIAL MEDIA MARKETING

Created by Aristotle and popularised by some of today's best thinkers like Elon Musk, 'First-principles' thinking is a mindset that helps us unlock our creativity and inspiration.

Typically our ideas are constrained by what has gone before. This is typically as a result of our experiences in childhood. Much of what we believe to be true is based on an 'authority' figure telling us that something is so.

From our earliest days, we are taught to stop questioning and are trained on compliance and acceptance. This impacts our thought processes in later life, leaving us to rely on our emotions, or our 'gut' to make decisions.

Fundamentally, if we never learn to take something apart, test the assumptions, and reconstruct it, we end up trapped in what other people tell us — trapped in the way things have always been done.

First-principles helps us see beyond the status quo. We can see the rules that govern the state of play and as a result, we can see what is possible.

Essentially, most things just shared beliefs. Money is a shared belief. So is a border. So is ownership. The list goes on.

One of the best ways to establish a first-principles mindset is to use 'Socratic questioning' to challenge existing beliefs to get to the core of what is true and what is unknown.

Socratic questioning generally follows this process:[15]

1. What exactly do I think and why do I think this?
2. How do I know this is true? What if I thought the opposite?
3. How can I back this up? What are the sources?
4. What might others think? How do I know I am correct?
5. What if I am wrong? What are the consequences if I am?
6. Why did I think that? Was I correct? What conclusions can I draw from the this process?

---

[15] https://fs.blog/first-principles/

This process stops you from relying too heavily on emotional responses. It takes a scientific approach which is predicated on disproving a hypothesis.

In fact, that's a key difference between how scientists and marketers operate. Scientists work to prove themselves wrong and marketers work to prove themselves right. This second approach opens up the risk of 'confirmation bias' and links the outcome (whether something was wrong or right) to our ego and the act of proving ourselves right.

Unsurprisingly, this limits our learning and means we can't think in a first-principles way. This is how Elon Musk describes first-principles thinking: [16]

"I think people's thinking process is too bound by convention or analogy to prior experiences. It's rare that people try to think of something on a first principles basis. They'll say, "We'll do that because it's always been done that way." Or they'll not do it because "Well, nobody's ever done that, so it must not be good. But that's just a ridiculous way to think. You have to build up the reasoning from the ground up—"from the first principles" is the phrase that's used in physics. You look at the fundamentals and construct your reasoning from that, and then you see if you have a conclusion that

[16] Elon Musk, quoted by Tim Urban in "The Cook and the Chef: Musk's Secret Sauce," Wait But Why https://waitbutwhy.com/2015/11/the-cook-and-the-chef-musks-secret-sauce.html

works or doesn't work, and it may or may not be different from what people have done in the past."

Taking Musk's reasoning and applying it to social media, here are what I deem as the 6 fundamentals of social media marketing.

1. Scaling 'word of mouth' is our ultimate ambition

Encouraging your customers to share their positive experiences is the most efficient way to grow a business. The network effects of social media enables word of mouth to spread faster than ever before.

2. Collaboration increases opportunity

When we work with others we reach new audiences.

3. Participation increases engagement

People don't care about brands, they care about themselves. Participation gives people a reason to care and a reason to engage.

4. Engagement drives reach

Platforms change continually, but the one principle that remains consistent is that the more people that interact with your posts, the more people your posts will be shown to.

5. Reach drives awareness

The rule of seven[17] dictates that prospects need to see a message seven times before they gain cognitive awareness. Reaching more people more often increases your influence.

6. In most peoples eyes, the 'best product' is the one they know

Our job in marketing is to maximise 'mental availability', being the first brand that comes to mind when a customer requires a solution.

The six fundamentals will be explored in more depth throughout this book and sit at the core of the SOCIAL 3.0 framework.

Let's now get into the '6C's' of the framework, starting with our 'Customer'.

---

[17] https://www.krusecontrolinc.com/rule-of-7-how-social-media-crushes-old-school-marketing-2021/

CUSTOMER

CONTEXT

CREATIVITY

COMMUNITY

CHANNELS

CALCULATION

CHAPTER 5

CREATING YOUR AUDIENCE. HOW TO RETHINK MARKET ORIENTATION

"There is only one boss. The customer. And she can fire everybody in the company from the CEO on down, simply by spending her money somewhere else." - Sam Walton, founder, Walmart.

Let's begin by talking about focus. Of course, most of us want to reach the biggest possible audience, to be seen by millions, to maximise return on investment and to have a huge impact.

But, in order to appeal to as many people as possible, we end up making compromises, we dumb it down and average it out.

When you seek to appeal to everyone, you'll rarely delight anyone.

The solution is simple but counterintuitive: Find the smallest market that can sustain your business. When you get focussed on a small set of customers that all share the same challenges, frustrations, ambitions and worldviews, your story and the impact you'll make all go up by an order of magnitude.

Seth Godin refers to this as the 'Minimum Viable Audience' [18] and it's something we applied in the early days of growing ContentCal. Here's a short, personal story;

In mid 2016, we were pre-launch of ContentCal and we had one 'beta' customer that was the former employer of the ContentCal founder and CEO, Alex. This business was a large multinational enterprise business and as such, the feedback they were providing to us in terms of product development was very much through a large business lens.

Based on this, we were beginning to think we must be an enterprise level product. We then decided to approach

---

[18] https://seths.blog/2017/07/in-search-of-the-minimum-viable-audience/

similar large businesses, sharing the experiences and learnings from our first beta customer. All we found were closed doors.

Back to the drawing board. We spent 3 further months meeting with companies of all different industries and sizes sharing our vision and listening intently. We began to see some patterns emerging in small marketing agencies gravitating towards the vision of what we were creating.

We weren't fully committed to this target customer yet, so in December 2016, six months after winning our first beta client we decided to launch the product as a self-serve business, where anyone could sign up for a free trial and we created some basic messaging to appeal to a wide audience.

When you let potential customers self-select in this way, it's incredibly powerful for a number of reasons.

Firstly, if you build it, they don't come. We overestimated the impact of a 'launch day'. Secondly, your early expectations of growth will be way off. In most cases, things take 10 times longer than you expect or hope them to. But thirdly, and most importantly, 'launch day' is when the real learning starts. We began to see patterns in conversion, again mirroring this small agency group.

We then pivoted our growth strategy to focus on small agencies and social media freelancers. This group had the same pains of a shared hatred for spreadsheet-based content calendars and the relentless chasing of clients for content approvals. What made this group particularly appealing is that nearly everyone had cobbled together their own solution to try and solve their pain. When people have felt the pain so significantly and not found a way to solve it, that they've had to create their own solution, you know that you are on to the perfect market fit and an ideal minimum viable audience.

The key word here is compromise. For a product that has mass market applicability to only focus on one customer group might seem like a missed opportunity. However, your minimum viable audience does not need to mean the only audience you'll ever target. Consider your minimum viable audience as the kindling that sparks the fire of word of mouth. This approach helps your reputation spread into increasingly large audiences that will sustain your business over the long term.

In the words of Steve Jobs:

"People think focus means saying 'yes' to the thing you've got to focus on. But that's not what it means at all. It means saying 'no' to the hundred other good ideas that there are. You have to pick carefully. I'm actually as proud of the things we haven't done as the things I have done."[19]

This is what Step 1 of the SOCIAL 3.0 Framework is all about. The user persona, finding their pains, and understanding what they have done to try and solve this pain.

So, how do we go about finding this minimum viable audience?

We need to ask ourselves some questions that might seem simple, but they require some deep thinking.

1. What change do you seek to make?

Every organisation is a change maker, it's our job to change behaviours to unlock opportunities for customers.

---

[19] https://bettermarketing.pub/find-your-minimum-viable-audience-f57c404dd612

This question needs to link intrinsically to your purpose or your 'why', as we discussed earlier.

Going back to the ContentCal example from earlier:

'We believe in the power of connection. Connections create communities, and strong communities create unstoppable businesses.'

2. Who's it for?

In my personal view, user persona documents are where a marketer's logic goes to die. I've been there too, but over time you realise that thinking that someone makes a decision because they are called Susan, aged 35, has two cats and lives in Manhattan is utter nonsense.

Psychographics over demographics every time. Demographics are a rough approximation and a way of averaging things out, which as we discussed earlier, when we try to get mass appeal by averaging things out it is a sure fire way to appeal to precisely no one. Psychographics allows us to think about the human emotions that impact our buyers, for example;

- What do they care about?
- What is their shared worldview?

- What challenges do they face?
- How have they tried to solve these challenges?
- What keeps them up at night?
- What are they afraid of?

At this point, we just want to note down what we *believe* the answers to these questions are for our target buyer — this is just a hypothesis. These answers will help us create a '*problem statement*' for our chosen minimum viable audience.

To give you the ContentCal example:

Persona:
Small social media agencies and freelancers

Problem Statement:
Creating quality content takes significant time. Most of this time is wasted on a disjointed spreadsheet-based content creation workflow and chasing client approvals.

With a hypothesis of our persona and the problem statement, it's time to craft our value proposition that transforms our problem statement into a story that will resonate with our target audience.

CUSTOMER

CONTEXT

CREATIVITY

COMMUNITY

CHANNELS

CALCULATION

CHAPTER 6

CREATING A VALUE PROPOSITION. HOW TO USE DATA TO CRAFT THE RIGHT MESSAGE

It's a popular saying currently that an organisation is 'data-driven'. But I'm not so sure that's something you'd want to brag about, certainly not in a market-orientated, customer-focussed business.

Firstly, 'data' means nothing without a story to give context to the numbers (something we will explore more later in this book). Secondly, as we've covered so far in this book, it's clear there is little logic when it comes to buying decisions, with the true reasons behind preferences and purchases often hidden in the subconscious and the emotional state of our target audience.

Personally, I advocate for a *'data-informed'* approach as opposed to one that is governed solely by what the numbers say. In this approach we balance both objective and subjective information to arrive at the right value proposition that will resonate with our target audience.

As we've already got a hypothesis of our persona and problem statement, we need to add some research to support, or disprove this. Disproving a hypothesis is an important part of the process, being mindful to not be caught up by 'confirmation bias' whereby we only search and find information that supports our beliefs.

To validate (or indeed invalidate) the hypothesis of our target audiences' problem statement, we're going to conduct this research in three parts.

1. Your data

If you are already serving this target audience, we can start by looking into our data and asking ourselves some questions:

- What persona has the shortest sales cycle?
- What persona pays the most?
- What persona has the best conversion rate?

- What persona has the best retention rate?
- What persona do we delight the most?
- What persona talks about us the most?

Hopefully, the answer to these questions will show a trend towards a clear persona. For each of the above questions, the key is to ask 'why?'. We need to go beneath the surface to try and find the reasons and meaning behind the answers.

After asking yourself these questions, take a look into your past content performance (social media, webinars, blogs etc.) and look at what content has performed the best. What topic was it? What was the theme? What persona has engaged with the content?

2. Your competitors

Whether you have begun serving this audience or not, taking a peek into what your competitors are doing will give you additional insight to inform your value proposition.

The best place to look is in your competitors' social content. Again, what posts are working well for them? What platforms are they posting them on? What format are they posting them in (Image, carousel or video etc.)? What type of topics are they talking about? What hashtags are they using? What are people saying in the comments?

All of this data is easily found by browsing through your competitors' feeds or using one of the many social media analytics tools that are out there on the market.

3. Your market

With an understanding of what's worked for both us and our competitors, we now need to look at the broader market in this third and final approach to market research.

The best way to do this is to find communities where your target audience gathers, like Facebook groups, Reddit or on Discord. Social media is becoming increasingly fragmented into microcosms of subcultures, led by creators that are building communities around their niche. You can find groups and communities for pretty much anything now and this presents an incredible opportunity to gain insight into our audience at a scale that would never have been possible before.

Once you've found these communities, spend time following the threads of conversation — what are people saying? What challenges keep on coming to light? What words are they using? Start becoming an active member in these groups, asking questions which will help you unlock further understanding. However, be sure to operate in these groups with a mindset of contribution — always add value before you look to extract value.

Pro Tip: In my experience, having a podcast is the single best way to meet and ask in-depth questions to those individuals that you really want to know more about. It's an approach that leads with generosity (giving someone else a stage), helps you gather new insights and creates great content in the process. A true win-win-win.

In addition to the qualitative feedback from your target audiences' communities, we now need to gain some additional quantitative intelligence based on our target audiences' search habits and trends. This will give us a clear 360 degree picture of what our target audience cares about and will ensure we have the most balanced approach to market research.

Market Research Tools

We all love tools in marketing and fortunately we have no shortage of choice. Here are my recommended six tools to use to ensure we capture the quantitative insights we need to craft our value proposition and inform our creative output.

1. Keyword Strategy Tool

One of the best tools for understanding our target's search habits is www.keywordstrategytool.com. Using this tool you can view what your target audience is searching for on Google and YouTube - the two primary channels people use to research.

On this tool, you can search against different terms that you think your target audience might be searching for. This will bring back a series of results, out of which we can filter the key questions your audience are asking and the volume of searches against each question.

This gives us incredibly valuable insight into the minds of our target audience and what they are seeking to understand. But also, what we've also got here is absolute gold in terms of content marketing, because these are the questions that people want answered. And if we're looking to build trust, we want to answer people's questions through the content we create.

2. Answer the Public

As an additional tool to support the findings of www.keywordstrategytool.com, I would recommend www.answerthepublic.com — this creates a wonderful graphic of the clusters of topics your audience are searching for. The visual display is better than the Keyword Strategy Tool, but lacks the numerical evidence.

3. Google Data Search

If you are looking for statistics to support a campaign, this can be a useful tool to aggregate all of the supporting research that can provide the evidence to help inform your target audience research and for your content ideas.

4. Exploding Topics

A fantastic tool to look at emerging trends and the growth of these topics. Exploding topics gives you another dimension to consider in both your market research and to help inspire creativity.

5. Buzzsumo

This tool is wonderful for seeing the specific content that is performing well in your category, along with what channels and on which publications. This works nicely in conjunction with Exploding Topics, with Exploding Topics representing the high-level, topic-based trends and Buzzsumo supporting this by surfacing the specific content that is driving the growth of these topics.

6. Social Media Listening

In this final piece of quantitative analysis, I would recommend using a social media listening tool (there are many on the market). This will help you understand the things people are saying about you, your competitors and your category across social media, along with the typical sentiment of the audience.

With a beautiful balance of both qualitative and quantitative analysis of our data, our competitors and our market, against our persona's problem statement, we've now got the data to both validate and help us shape our Problem Statement.

Returning back to the ContentCal example, based on our minimum viable audience of Small social media agencies and freelancers, let's now see how the initial Problem Statement has evolved:

Small social media agencies and freelancers…

- *…care about creating content they are proud of*
- *…care about getting results for their clients*
- *…feel under-appreciated by clients*
- *…feel frustrated with the time it takes to create content*
- *…feel burned out with the relentless need to churn out creative content*
- *…are frustrated by disjointed content creation workflow*
- *…waste time chasing client approvals.*
- *… are kept awake at night by the ever-changing world of social media and being left-behind*
- *… are worried about the negative impact that managing social media content has on their personal lives*

As you can see, we've now got a much clearer picture of what the target audience truly cares about and we've rooted our qualitative research in objective data.
To shape our value proposition, we're now ready to answer the 3rd question further to the two we asked earlier;

- What change do we seek to make?
- Who's it for?
- **What's it for?**

This is the 'how' of Simon Sinek's Golden Circle we covered earlier. This involves framing your product or service in the context of the audience we are seeking to serve and the change we are seeking to make.

If we go back to our problem statement, we can begin to link to a specific outcome.

Small social media agencies and freelancers…

- *…care about creating content they are proud of* > ***Create better content***
- *…care about getting results for their clients* > ***Increase impact***
- *…feel under-appreciated by clients* > ***Demonstrate value***
- *…feel frustrated with the time it takes to create content* > ***Save time***
- *…feel burned out with the relentless need to churn out creative content* > ***Save time***
- *…are frustrated by disjointed content creation workflow* > ***Simplify processes***

- *…waste time chasing client approvals.* **> Simplify processes**
- *… are kept awake at night by the ever-changing world of social media and being left-behind* **> Become part of a community**
- *… are worried about the negative impact that managing social media content has on their personal lives* **> Save time**

No one cares about your brand, they care about themselves. We need to simply frame what our product does in the context of what our customers are about.

We now bring these three points into a 'value proposition' which would look something like this:

'We believe in the power of connection. Connections create communities, and strong communities create unstoppable businesses. Small social media agencies and freelancers get this, striving to achieve this everyday for their clients.

But, the relentless need to create meaningful content is incredibly challenging, impacting time spent with family and finding themselves stuck in a constant battle with clients to help them understand the long-term impact of social media.

At ContentCal, we've been there and we get it. We help businesses build long-lasting communities through simple, yet powerful social media tools and provide access to a community of like minded social media professionals that care about improving both their own learning and the results they get for clients.'

We now truly understand our target audience and can now speak the language that will resonate.

But, success here is all about 'focus'. Simply put, you cannot please everyone. You have to decide which persona makes sense to target for your business, but when you do decide, the story you can tell and the impact you make will be significantly improved.

With an understanding or our persona and their problem statement along with our value proposition, we're now ready for step 3 of the SOCIAL 3.0 Framework, Customer Discovery.

CUSTOMER

CONTEXT

CREATIVITY

COMMUNITY

CHANNELS

CALCULATION

CHAPTER 7

CUSTOMER DISCOVERY. HOW TO ENSURE YOUR MESSAGE RESONATES

This is where the 'rubber meets the road', as they say. This is the part where the research and hypotheses are battle-tested with potential or current customers for impact and resonance.

Customer Discovery is common to product development processes, but it is an element that's missing from so many marketing functions. It's a pet peeve of mine that marketing is meant to be the 'voice of the customer', yet they are often the function that spends the least time with them. This is a situation that needs to be resolved if we truly want our messages to cut through.

Conversations with actual people will tell you more than a spreadsheet ever could. In the Customer Discovery process, we want to recruit a small group (a minimum of seven) of prospects or customers with whom we can share our value proposition along with some draft campaign ideas and creative concepts to gauge if our hypotheses and research actually speaks the truth of our target persona.

Pro Tip: When interviewing, people are typically terrible at telling you what they really feel. A good way to 'hack' your way into getting salient feedback is to ask your customers to project their views about someone else. For example, questions like *'What do you think other social media freelancers struggle with the most?'* or *'What makes a good social media agency?'* will help you get more in-depth answers as it removes the filter we apply when we talk to new people from a personal perspective.

If our messages and ideas do not resonate, this is our opportunity to revisit the persona & problem statement step and pivot our hypothesis.

It might seem like a lot of work is going into the first three steps of this process, but getting the diagnosis and foundations right first makes the tactical execution so much easier, as we no longer need to worry if our story is right, we just need to consider the creative and channel. As we know, everything begins with the story.

Talking of stories, that's where we are heading next.

CHAPTER 8
TELLING STORIES.
USING STORYTELLING TO UNLOCK CREATIVITY

In general, people don't believe what you tell them. In fact, they rarely believe what you show them. But, they often believe what their friends tell them and they always believe what they tell themselves. And what's at the core of what people tell themselves?

A story.

In this chapter we'll cover storytelling and how you can create a narrative around your brand.

The purpose of marketing is to cause change. If we're trying to build a movement, raise money, sell a product, change lifestyles, build community—these are all marketing activities that exist to change the way people act.

Changing behaviour does not happen as a result of rational evidence, if we want to change behaviour we need to change the story.

To give you the perfect example of the power of a story, In 2009 an experiment, called the 'Significant Objects' was conducted to demonstrate that the effect of a story on any given object's subjective value can be measured objectively.

The project auctioned off thrift-store objects via eBay; for item descriptions, short stories were purpose-written by over 200 contributing writers, including were substituted. The objects, purchased for $1.25 apiece on average, sold for nearly $8,000.00 in total, a profit of 2,700% [20]

This is wonderful the science of storytelling in full effect.

---

[20] https://significantobjects.com/

Presentations expert David JP Phillips gives a wonderful TED talk on the magical science of storytelling [21], in which he explains that when we are on the receiving end of a story, chemicals in our brain act to suspend our critical thinking.

When we are truly engrossed in a story, our brain releases Dopamine, which improves focus, motivation and memory — all feelings you want to introduce when selling to someone. Stories that are emotionally intense generate Oxytocin which increases generosity, trust and bonding - facilitating an emotional connection. Again, important factors in helping an audience connect with your message. And when you make people laugh with a story, even in a gentle way, this stimulates the production of Endorphins which encourages creativity, focus and relaxation, Phillips calls this mix of emotions, the 'Angels cocktail'

When telling a story, build suspense and create a cliffhanger — this will trigger Dopamine for the recipient, empowering their focus and memory. If your objective is to build trust, tell a personal and emotional story. This will

---

[21] https://www.youtube.com/watch?v=Nj-hdQMa3uA0)

trigger Oxytocin, known as the 'love drug', building empathy for the recipient.

With a baseline understanding of the importance of storytelling, let's now focus on storytelling structures. Whilst there are many storytelling structures out there, I'm going to call out Diane Wiredu's 'Triple-S' messaging framework.[22]

As we've already covered, at the heart of messaging is connection. Your story IS your strategy, so we need our story to precede all of our tactics.

The art of storytelling is in finding the right words for the right people and putting them in the right order, for this we'll use the 'Triple-S' messaging framework

Triple-S Messaging Framework

1. Story

The story (or narrative) is that fundamental truth that your company lives by. This is your 'why' at the centre of the Golden Circle.

---

[22] https://themarketingmeetup.com/events/how-to-find-the-right-message-diane-wiredu/

Your 'why' will have become clear from the first three steps we've already covered, in persona and problem statement, value proposition and customer discovery.

However, we want to establish our brand archetype, which will help frame our story.

There are multiple archetypes we could work with; of which the following archetype model demonstrates. All archetypes spiralling from the four foundations of:

- Belonging
- Structure
- Legacy
- Independence

We need to associate our business to one of these archetypes and we need to 'own' that archetype throughout all of our messaging across all channels, so it needs to be one that feels authentic for us and appealing for our audience. [23]

---

[23] https://medium.com/ebaqdesign/brand-archetypes-the-ultimate-guide-with-48-examples-44b39eb41c8f

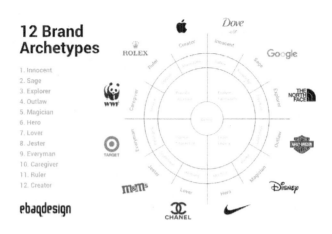

12 Brand Archetypes

1. Innocent
2. Sage
3. Explorer
4. Outlaw
5. Magician
6. Hero
7. Lover
8. Jester
9. Everyman
10. Caregiver
11. Ruler
12. Creator

ebaqdesign

Using these archetypes, we can frame our 'why'. For example;

- Patagonia: Force for good
  - "We care. We stand for something bigger. Together, let's change the world."

- TransferWise (Wise): Peoples' savior
  - "You're being treated unfairly. We're gonna put a stop to it. We stand up for what's right!"

2. Structure

Building on our understanding of our audience, we can now structure our story in a way that it will trigger the 'Angels' cocktail' of emotions that we spoke of earlier.

One of the most popular models for this is Freytag's pyramid;

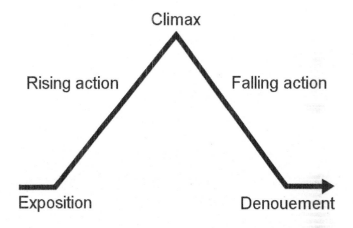

- Exposition - The situation today
- Rising action - The vision and the view of a better world
- Climax - The challenge that prevents progression
- Falling action - The killer insight that leads us to a better tomorrow

- Denouement - The idea that unlocks this opportunity

With an understanding of how to structure our message, we now need to shape this into the structure of our communications.

3. Shape

Finally, we need to shape and define our message. We can do this by evaluating what our prospect is thinking and their thought processes.

- "Who the heck are you? And what do you do?"
  - **Headline and your 'why'**
- "Cool, but what's in it for me?"
  - **Customer-Focused Value Proposition**
- "Can I trust you?"
  - **Social Proof/Consensus**
- "Okay… Show me then. How do you do it?"
  - **'How' your solution solves the challenge**
- "Okay… But why should I care about this?"
  - **'Describe why it's important now**
- "Why should I believe you?"
  - **Social Proof**

- "What do I get?"
  - **'What' you do**
- "Alright. What should I do next?"
  - **Call to Action**

We've covered a lot so far: the importance of a brand, buyer psychology, finding our audience and their pains, doing the market research and crafting our value proposition, validating the proposition through customer discovery and using these insights to craft a story. But we could condense that last 40 pages into just 2 paragraphs.

How marketing works for unremarkable businesses

Find a large group of people.

Explain why you're better.

Prove that you are the right answer.

Done.

How remarkable companies approach marketing

Find the right audience.

Understand what they care about.

Tell a story.

Deliver a service that feels like it was made for them.

They spread the word.

CUSTOMER

CONTEXT

CREATIVITY

COMMUNITY

CHANNELS

CALCULATION

CHAPTER 9

SETTING OBJECTIVES.

CREATING MEASURABLE SOCIAL

MEDIA GOALS

Many people talk about the "blurred line" between Sales & Marketing, but as the CEO of Refine Labs, Chris Walker [24] puts it, the line is super clear.

Personally, I feel B2B marketing functions need to make the following definition crystal clear to their leadership teams, as a mindset shift needs to occur for B2B's to truly unlock the potential of marketing.

Here's the definition:

----

[24] https://www.linkedin.com/in/chris-walker-41597028/

Sales = I'm trying to convert someone **now**.

Marketing = I'm trying to educate someone to build trust and connection for the **future**

Based on that definition:

- Most marketers actually mainly execute Sales (lead generation & supporting sales).
- Performance "marketing" is actually Sales.
- Direct response "marketing" is actually Sales.

To be clear, it's not a bad thing for Marketers to execute Sales. But, what's important is that leadership and marketing teams recognise the percentage of time, effort and budget that's allocated to these definitions of Marketing vs. Sales.

According to research from the Ehrenberg-Bass institute, the majority of an available market does *not* have the intent to buy (95%). And for that segment, the best option is to execute *marketing*.

But really what many B2B brands continue to do is treat marketing as sales support and task them to deliver sales-oriented activity to appeal to the tiny segment of a market (5%) that actually want to buy now.

We need to readdress that balance as a matter of urgency and that means not judging a marketing function's success solely on lead generation targets. Let's be honest, numbers like this are easy to game and at best, only drive short term results.

This type of behaviour doesn't happen in B2C. Consumer focussed businesses appreciate the impact of marketing and the importance of brand. For example, Coke's marketers are not crazy enough to think they need to compete with Pepsi on features (the product delusion). Coke knows it competes, and wins, on stronger mental and physical availability (the market reality).

It's not just B2C's that get this though, some forward-thinking B2B get the importance of a brand-first approach too. Take Salesforce's feral racoon child, Astro[25], it doesn't communicate the specs of its CRM software. And yet, Astro works wonders, helping Salesforce dominate its category year after year.

---

[25] https://www.marketingweek.com/brand-characters-b2b-marketing/

A growing number of marketers recognise the limitations of the product-first approach. But there's a bigger problem: at most B2B organisations, marketing doesn't actually run marketing. Sales, finance and product run marketing, and branding doesn't fit in their spreadsheets.

But, it doesn't need to be this way — as marketers and business leaders we need to be clearer about the impact marketing has on a business over the long term and set objectives that drive the right behaviours.

Setting objectives

Setting objectives need not be complex. Often in marketing we do our best to overcomplicate what should be simple. For example, if we look at the marketing funnel, there are really only five things that we're ever out to achieve:

1. Awareness

We're seeking to get our messages and brand seen by as many people as possible.

2. Consideration

We're seeking to build trust and affinity with our audience

3. Conversion

We're seeking for someone to take action

4. Loyalty

We're trying to make people love us and stay with us

5. Advocacy

We're trying to make our offering so powerful that it benefits our audience to tell others.

Every objective we set within marketing will fall within one of these stages of the marketing funnel. Mostly, objectives will be centred around the top three.

As we've already discussed however, we need to be wary of focussing marketing objectives on the 'conversion' stage of the funnel, which is actually a 'sales' job, not 'marketing'. Of course, I'm not suggesting we should remove any lead generation targets from marketing, but we need to prioritise it correctly alongside brand and engagement building.

Like we said earlier, 60% of the budget should go on brand building, with 40% on short-term sales conversion activity.

This then makes objective setting even easier, as we are now only focussing on the top two stages of the funnel. It's essential however that the objectives that we set within a marketing function align with the objectives that we are setting at an organisational level.

For example, if one of the businesses' ambitions is to 'become number one in the market', we need to ensure that this objective is mirrored in our marketing objectives, and importantly, we make this objective quantifiable. Thinking in this way will help marketers speak the language of the C-Suite, ensuring that marketing is seen as the key vehicle to drive this growth alongside sales and product.

If we take this objective of 'becoming number one', and break it down, the first step in becoming 'number one' is always going about to be getting in front of more people and as a result, increasing our *Share of Voice*.

This is when we can return back to our marketing funnel and start to consider the 'metrics that matter' related to each objective. We don't want track everything, but there's typically a few 'metrics that matter' within each stage of the funnel, as shown below.

In addition to some examples of the 'metrics that matter' on the left, on the right hand side of the above graphic, you'll see 'followers, likes and comments'. I've put these here as we often fixate on these in a social media context, but I'd class these as 'vanity metrics' — metrics that are unrelated to a business objective.

These metrics are helpful for us to gauge the health of our accounts, but realistically they don't tell us if we're getting any closer to hitting our objective. In my view, this has been one of the main reasons that social media marketing and social media marketers in general have and, in some cases, continue to be underpaid and under-appreciated within B2B organisations. I see an opportunity to change that if we can align social media goals with business growth ambitions.

Going back to this example objective of 'becoming number one', there are really two 'metrics that matter'. Firstly, 'Share of Voice'. I find this metric massively underused in a B2B setting. Share of Voice relates to the volume of conversation that your brand is part of. You can pull share of voice analysis very easily from most social media listening tools, like www.mentionlytics.com and can compare the volume of conversation that your brand is part of and map that against your competition.

Increasing your share of voice is critical to growing your market share. As a result, it should be a key metric in demonstrating our progress towards our objective of 'becoming number one'.

The graphic on the following page demonstrates the impact of your 'Share of Voice' perfectly. If your share of voice is larger than your share of your market, then your brand will grow. If your share of voice is lower than your market share, your brand will shrink.

For me, this is a perfect way of visualising the impact of brand level marketing on business growth. It's these dynamics that are often hidden from leadership teams of businesses or misunderstood hence we see many leadership teams to defaulting marketing success metrics that they can measure easily, like leads.

If you aren't reaching more customers than you have, **you cannot grow.**

However, the limitation of share a voice is that this analysis is not actionable. Share of voice data is very valuable to analyse and track progress of every quarter, but we also need another more actionable metric that can help us track our progress on a more day-by-day, week-by-week and month-by-month basis.

The metric for us to consider in addition is 'impressions'. 'Impressions' metric relates to the amount of times your content has been seen and is relevant across multiple channels. This allows us to break down our marketing performance across our marketing site, search ads, display, paid social, organic social, website content etc. using a single metric (impressions) to understand our growth across all channels.

More impressions leads to more awareness, more awareness leads to more engagement, more engagement results in an increase in share of voice and an increase in share of voice relates to an increase in market share.

This is just an example of one objective, and two metrics to track, but hopefully this simplifies and clarifies how we should set objectives and define success in B2B marketing.

Key takeaways for setting objectives and measuring metrics:

- Set meaningful marketing objectives that think beyond short term lead generation

- Brand building should take 60% of the marketing budget and resource, the remaining 40% should be focussed on lead generation — try and get the whole business on board with that focus.

- Ensure marketing objectives are aligned with the overall business objective

- Understand and ensure the rest of the organisation appreciates the importance of share of voice

We're now at the stage of the process where we can now turn our hand to strategy creation. We've completed the 'diagnosis' by establishing our persona and problem statement, validated our value proposition and market research through customer discovery, have crafted our story and now know what we are out to achieve.

Ready for the fun bit? Let's turn our hand to creativity.

CHAPTER 10

QUALITATIVE CREATIVITY.

CREATING CONTENT PILLARS

Over the coming three chapters, we're going to the cover the three sides of what I call the 'The Creativity Triangle'

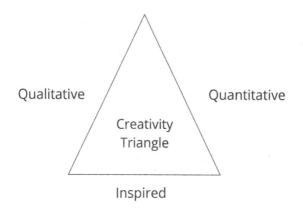

Qualitative creativity focuses on using our objective learnings from our persona, problem statement, value proposition and customer discovery work and using this to come up with creative concepts.

Quantitative creativity calls on some of the market research tools we introduced earlier to gain data-backed insights that will help steer our creativity

Inspired creativity is more serendipitous and unlocks new possibilities by watching trends and involving more people in the creative process.

Before we dive into Qualitative creativity, there are 6 golden rules for creativity. These rules have been inspired by Eddie Shelyner of VeryGoodCopy [26]

6 Golden rules of creativity

- 'Connectivity' is a better word than 'Creativity'. Don't put pressure on yourself to be truly original. Very little truly is. The key is in connecting existing ideas in new ways.

---

[26] https://www.verygoodcopy.com/

- Be an idiot. The secret to being good at anything is to approach it like a curious idiot, rather than a know-it-all genius. Pretending we have all the answers limits our possibility.

- Step away from your devices. John Cleese once said: "We don't know where we get our ideas from. What we do know is that we do not get them from our laptops."

- Learn to listen intently. You don't need to have great ideas, when you can hear great ideas.

- Write it all down. Ideas are often forgotten as quickly as they come, set yourself up with a place to store all of your ideas, no matter how far-fetched they might be

- Forget it. Once you've written it down, let your conscious mind forget it. Let your unconscious mind do the work. This is when those 'lightbulb moments' happen.

Sometimes I feel that the word creativity is quite loaded. Often you'll see the word 'creative' next to words like 'genius'.

I feel that sometimes that creates an unrealistic expectation of what we're trying to achieve through our marketing content.

With 'creativity', and the three ways that we're going to be looking at it, all we're trying to achieve is to have a continual pool of ideas and inspiration that we can call on to ensure that we create the best possible content that will have the best chance of resonating with our audience.

When we consider social content, typically, it needs to achieve one or multiple of three ambitions.

- To educate
- To inspire
- To entertain

Remember, on social media channels we are competing with pictures of cats, not with our competitors. Our job is to stop the scroll and capture attention by offering content that's either useful or entertaining.

When thinking about creativity and in the beginnings of a content strategy, I find 'education' content the easiest to start with. Educational content is a key part of the B2B content mix because when you educate someone, you add value, when you add value you build trust, and trust is what builds a brand. So you can see how education content should really be a cornerstone of any B2B's, social media content strategy.

In the problem statement, value proposition and customer development steps, we'll have already got a clear idea of who our customers are, and their unique challenges. This will have given us important insight into the types of educational content we want to create for our audience.

At ContentCal, we leaned into education as a core part of our content strategy. To bring this to life, let's go back to our persona and problem statements from earlier:

Small social media agencies and freelancers…

- *…care about creating content they are proud of*
- *…care about getting results for their clients*
- *…feel under-appreciated by clients*
- *…feel frustrated with the time it takes to create content*
- *…feel burned out with the relentless need to churn out creative content*
- *…are frustrated by disjointed content creation workflow*
- *…waste time chasing client approvals.*
- *… are kept awake at night by the ever-changing world of social media and being left-behind*

- *... are worried about the negative impact that managing social media content has on their personal lives*

From these challenges we can begin to see some key themes emerging:

- Ideation
- Creation
- Process & Workflow
- Collaboration
- Publishing
- Optimization
- Analysis

You'll notice that themes mirror a social media agencies/ freelancers process, so it ensures that we create educational content that supports them every step of the way.

With these topics in mind, we can then think about the different formats we have at our disposal. As we mentioned in the '6 golden rules of creativity', creativity is more about 'connection' that it is creating something from scratch, and sometimes a new idea can be spun out of putting the same creative concept into a different 'content type'.

These content types could be:

- Social feed (image/video/carousel)
- Social story
- Blog
- Email
- Content Download
- Webinar
- Video
- Podcast
- Ebook
- Whitepaper
- Guides
- Livestream
- AMA / Q&A
- Academy
- Community/Group

At ContentCal, the focal point was our webinars. Although in total, we leant on five different content types

- Webinar
- Guides
- Blog
- Video

All of the education material that we delivered across each of these formats was linked together in our 'Academy', which created a structured learning journey for users, along with accreditation.

Pro Tip: The academy approach takes some effort, but it's incredible the impact that accreditations have on encouraging users to consume all of the content. This approach is also viral by nature as those that complete the courses and get the certificates are encouraged to share this on social media, (of which many gladly do), which, in turn, encourages more people to participate. Academies can become scalable growth engines in themselves and at ContentCal we saw significant improvements in new customer acquisition and customer retention through this approach.

We can now map our themes with our chosen content types to see where our missed opportunities are, like this:

Themes	Ideate	Create	Process & Workflow	Collab	Publish	Analyse
Content Type						
Webinar	X	X	X		X	X
Blog	X	X	X	X		
Guide		X				X
Short Course	X			X		
Academy	X	X	X	X	X	X

Now we have our themes and content types mapped, this content will get distributed across multiple channels, of which we'll cover in chapter 15. These themes will also be further informed by the quantitative research we'll cover in the next chapter.

Now that we've covered the educational content, we now want to turn our focus to 'inspiration' oriented content. Returning to our persona analysis, you'll remember that one of the things that kept our audience awake at night was 'keeping up with the constant changes of social media'.

To help address this, at ContentCal, we came up with a plan where every month we would do a live run through of everything that's happened in the world of social media. We decided to create this content in collaboration with another well known individual within the social media space to deliver that with us. This opened up the content to a wider audience and added a different voice into the mix, creating a really nice dynamic for the content. Collaboration is a key to unlock creativity, as we'll cover in the final part of the 'Creativity Triangle'.

In addition to these monthly webinars, we supplemented this monthly update with a bitesize weekly social media update published on social channels. Again, you can see how the core idea has not changed, but the format has.

Over time, this format got increasingly popular and it grew into something that we became known for. Becoming 'known for something' is a cornerstone of building a brand and maximises 'mental availability' in the minds of your audience, meaning you become the first brand that comes to mind when they are looking for a solution.

Our themes and topics template can now evolve to factor in 'News' as an additional theme and 'Social' as an additional format.

Themes	Ideate	Create	Process & Workflow	Collab	Publish	Analyse	News
Formats							
Webinar	X	X	X		X	X	X
Blog	X	X	X	X			X
Guide		X				X	
Short Course	X			X			
Academy	X	X	X	X	X	X	
Social	X	X	X	X	X	X	X

Now to 'Entertainment' value content.

Entertaining content in a B2B setting is often the one that eludes most brands and it's the thing that holds B2B's back from leveraging the opportunity of emerging social media platforms like TikTok.

Talking of B2B creativity on TikTok however, have a look at Zoom and Sage's accounts — they demonstrate that B2B most certainly has a place on the platform and some of the results are incredible, with view counts of some videos well into the millions.

Both of these brands put a comedic angle to everyday business things, that if you're a user of Zoom, or any online meeting software for that matter, you'll definitely get.

To share a ContentCal example, we created a concept called 'Confessions of a content marketer'. We noticed that there was an increasing frequency of people sharing their marketing blunders on social media, and let's be honest we've all been in that place where we've sent a mass email and realised after the fact that every email starts with 'Hi, [first_name]'.... We created a user generated content focused campaign that was orientated around empowering others to share their marketing mishaps.

Confessions of a content marketer was a non branded initiative, we even went to the lengths of creating a separate Instagram account for this campaign. We wanted this initiative to take on a life of its own. The Instagram account, as a result of being an independent channel grew significantly faster than our branded channel and began generating engagement with our ideal target audience.

We would then re-share the content from the 'Confessions' social channel to the ContentCal branded channels, so there was connection back to the brand.

Going back to the importance of emotional connection as we discussed at the beginning of the book, taking this approach to 'Entertainment' content helps people connect with the brand in a way that helps them feel seen and heard, understood and appreciated.

CUSTOMER
CONTEXT
CREATIVITY
COMMUNITY
CHANNELS
CALCULATION

CHAPTER 11
QUANTITATIVE CREATIVITY.
HARNESSING DATA-LED INSIGHT
FROM OUR CONTENT, OUR
COMPETITORS AND THE BROADER
MARKET

The next step is 'quantitative creativity'. In this step, we're going to revert to the market research tools that we shared earlier to gain some objective insight into the content we should create.

Using the same methodology that we did within the qualitative section, we're going to look at content in the same three ways;

- To educate
- To inspire
- To entertain

Again, let's begin with education. Here, we're going to return to Keyword Strategy Tool along with Anger The Public, both of which will start guiding you towards some search-orientated trends. Within each of these tools we'll type in our category (like 'social media', in the case of ContentCal) and we'll begin to see a list of search terms related to your category, organised by volume of searches.

We'll be looking to organise these search terms by user 'intent'. By 'intent' we are referring to what the user is looking to achieve, it could be education and guidance or it could be purchase.

For ContentCal, here's an example of how it might break down:

Education intent

- What is social media engagement rate?
- How do I grow my social media followers?
- What's the best time to post?
- Best content calendar template
- What are the demographics on social media channels?

Purchase intent

- Best social media tool
- Best social media scheduling tools 2022
- Best content tool

The 'purchase intent' aspect of this is best served through an SEO strategy, whereby we should be focussing on creating blogs that rank for these terms and looking at the articles that already perform well on search and reaching out to the author to see if they can feature your product.

For social media orientated content we'll be focussing on the brand-building elements and as such, we'll focus on the education and research elements. To return back to the ContentCal example and those five content types of;

- Webinar
- Guides
- Blog
- Video
- Academy

This is where the guides really came into their own. From the example list of search terms above, when we were looking at the volume of searches it was clear that one topic seemed to be searched above all others — and that was people searching for a social media content calendar template.

This presented us the perfect opportunity to create a simple, Excel-based content calendar template. We gated this piece of content behind an email capture and hosted it on our marketing site, ensuring the page it lived on referenced all of the key search terms. After a few months, it began ranking as one of the biggest traffic drivers for ContentCal, bringing in more traffic than our paid channels.

It's pretty ironic that the business we created to remove the need for spreadsheets in content marketing was now promoting a spreadsheet-based approach, and to be honest I was not comfortable doing this at first, but sometimes we need to our personal preferences aside. That said, whilst the content calendar download template did not covert many customers as a result of seeing the article, it was often the initial entry point for users to discover ContentCal and be educated on a better approach to content marketing planning.

Continuing through our keyword analysis from Keyword Strategy Tool and Answer The Public begins to show up even more trends and will surface many that did not come up in your customer discovery. We can then use these to further inform our content themes.

When you use broad terms like 'social media' or 'content marketing' in these keyword research tools, as opposed to specific terms like 'social media management tool', you'll begin to get insight that will provide even more creative routes.

For example, at ContentCal, some of the most broad popular search terms were;

- 'How do I improve my Instagram engagement rate?'
- 'What does an engagement rate mean?'
- 'How do I increase reach on Instagram?'

Understanding the sheer volume of search terms related to these searches helped us get a clear picture of the need for channel-specific education and as a result, 'How-To' orientated content became another core content theme.

Themes	Ideate	Create	Process & Workflow	Collab	Publish	Analyse	News	How-To
Content Types								
Webinar	X	X	X		X	X	X	X
Blog	X	X	X	X			X	X
Guide		X				X		X
Short Course	X			X				X
Academy	X	X	X	X	X	X		X
Social	X	X	X	X	X	X	X	X

Now that we've evaluated search volume, 'quantitative creativity' can also be further informed by our competition.

At ContentCal, we noticed that our competitors' content around analytics was doing particularly well. We already knew from our persona and problem statement that 'analytics' was going to be an important area. However, looking at what was working well for our competition in terms of their social media content helped further inspire our creativity. Our competitors were going deep into things like; 'how to interpret social media analysis' and 'how to set goals' and from doing analysis of our competitors' social media platforms, we noticed that there was a lot of engagement on that content.

That gave us the inspiration to build more content around the analytics theme, once again, rooting that creativity in quantitative analysis.

This goes back to that first point where sometimes we burden ourselves with 'creativity' thinking that we need to be truly original. We don't, often we just need to stay curious and connect things together. Connecting what we might see from our competitors with our own unique viewpoint and presenting that in a different format (a social video vs. a blog, for example) lowers the barrier to creativity and opens up more opportunity.

Now that we've covered 'educational' content from a qualitative perspective, let's look at 'Inspirational' content.

One of the best ways to leverage 'inspirational' content is by working in collaboration with others. We're going to cover 'influencers' in more detail in a later chapter, however if we want to inspire an audience at scale, we need to work with others.

At this point, we're going to bring in a new tool, called Hype Auditor (https://hypeauditor.com/en/). This tool allows you to search for influential individuals across multiple social media platforms and get a picture of how relevant an individual is for your category, their influence and their audience quality score.

Working with influencers is not just reserved for those with big budgets. It just requires a bit more creativity when you're working with limited budgets. I'll give you two examples. One individual we chose to work with at ContentCal, was Matt Navarra. [27] We discovered Matt through his vibrant social media Facebook Group. As an aside, Facebook Groups and Sub Reddits are two of the best places to both find those niche communities that you seek to serve and those that run those communities typically make for perfect partners.

Matt's group was focussed on social media news and updates, which tied in perfectly with one of our themes of 'social media news' that we highlighted earlier. Matt was

---

[27] https://www.linkedin.com/in/mattnavarra/?originalSubdomain=uk

already sharing these updates weekly through his email newsletter, so we took the opportunity to work with him to re-format his social media news updates into a live webinar. But rather than running this as a one-off 'hit and hope' partnership, we created it into a series of webinars, all of which were promoted across both our channels and Matt's to maximise audience engagement. As a result this series of three webinars generated over 1,500 leads, at a cost per lead (CPL) of £10 each, 80% less than our typical paid CPL.

Another example was an unpaid partnership with a group run by Laura Moore and Laura Davis of a Facebook Group called 'The Hub for Social Media Managers'. From doing our research in the 'value proposition' stage of the process, where we were validating our persona and problem statement hypothesis through market research, we discovered this group, which was entirely focussed on serving our minimum viable audience of small social media agencies and freelancers. We found multiple ways to exchange value, from giving the group owners free access to our product to creating educational content for them and providing discounted access for their group members. In return, we were shared regularly and often spoke on their livestreams.

For the final part of quantitative creativity, let's now look at 'entertainment' value content. This type of content is often lifted directly from inspiration from what we've seen elsewhere.

There are two tools that will help you accelerate quantitative-based entertainment value content. Firstly, Exploding Topics (www.explodingtopics.com), will allow you to see the trends at the topic level. I also recommend supplementing this with specific searches on Pinterest trends (www.trends.pinterest.com) and Snapchat trends (www.trends.snapchat.com), and because many trends start on TikTok, I suggest heading to the 'Discover' page, searching your category and seeing the types of content and hashtags that are performing well, along with the sounds that are trending too.

Next we're going to go into the topic-level of trend discovery, for this we're going to use Buzzsumo (www.buzzsumo.com). Buzzsumo shows you the content that is performing best across social platforms and will provide you with the perfect inspiration of content you can do your own take on, or just re-share.

In all of these approaches to 'quantitative creativity', we're not considering the fact that someone's always done something as a roadblock, we're understanding the theme and topic and then informing our own strategy with this inspiration.

For both of these qualitative and quantitative approaches I'd recommend setting up some form of 'ideas library' for us to save all of these ideas and inspiration to. You might want to store these in a tool of your choice, like Trello or just a simple Excel document. Whichever approach you take, storing your ideas as they come up into one centralised place is essential to sparking creativity and speeding up the creative process.

Talking of inspiration, that takes us nicely onto the final side of the 'creativity triangle', Inspired creativity,

CUSTOMER

CONTEXT

CREATIVITY

COMMUNITY

CHANNELS

CALCULATION

CHAPTER 12

INSPIRED CREATIVITY.

TAKING ADVANTAGE OF TREND AND EMPOWERING ORGANISATION-WIDE CREATIVITY

Inspired creativity is about creating a structure to maximise serendipity. Even though, by nature, this approach is about inspiration, we can still make it a deliberate process.

So, we'll consider it in the same three contexts as we have for the other two elements of the creativity triangle:

- To educate
- To inspire
- To entertain

Beginning with education, again this is the most simplistic approach and relates to you being at the forefront of changes within your industry and being seen at the source of truth when it comes to how to interpret these changes.

As an example, this is why the weekly and monthly social media updates became so popular at ContentCal - there's a lot of complexity in any industry and it's our job to cut through this with salience. You can see the impact it has on our target audience.

Alanah Light · 1st
Social Media Consultant & Trainer | Helping owner-mana...

That will be you and me both Beth.... Bell clicked! Thanks for these micro updates Andy – love them!

1d ···

Jake Potter (He/Him) · 1st
Head of Social Media at Colt Technology Services & Pride in Londo...

Wow, I hadn't thought about the Instagram videos! Will have to test it :) Thanks for another great video.

1d ···

Ewa Orczykowska (She/Her) · 1st
Marketing Executive at Liftshare and Mobilityways - On a mission t...

Thanks for this, Andy! Your roundups are so helpful 🖤

2d ···

Having a 'news and trends' theme as part of your creative strategy, ensures you are never short of content and are front of mind for your audience when they need guidance. An essential component of trust building.

It's an approach that B2B construction payment software company Payapps takes. They focus on education around the ever-changing legislation around payment in the construction industry. Over time this is what they have become known for and as a result are often invited to contribute to press articles and industry debates. Ultimately, share-ability what we are trying to achieve through our social media content, maximising our opportunity for earned media.

Now, let's pick up on content that's designed to 'inspire'. One of the most powerful contributors to creativity is collaboration with others. The best content is always created together, so this is our opportunity to ensure that all of your colleagues, partners and customers get the opportunity to suggest content ideas.

Ideas could be collected on something as simple as a Google Form, or through using a tool like ContentCal. In either approach you open up the opportunity for creativity to flourish by centralising the ideas from a broader collective into a shared library of inspiration, ideally the same ideas library that we suggested earlier. In either approach, you unlock creativity through collaboration with a broader community.

Talking of organisation-wide creativity, Rich Burn, head of content for a Local Enterprise Partnership says; *'I have always thought "collaboration" is something to be explored more. With algorithms and SEO driving a lot of content strategy for many, is there a space for a "content reservoir" where like minded individuals can connect on like minded content and utilise the content for mutual gains.'*

These content suggestions might be from your employees that want to share common customer challenges, customer success stories or celebrations of an employees achievement.

Collaboration doesn't have to be limited internally either. External collaboration is often overlooked but is a crucial element. Customers and users should be encouraged and incentivised to share their success and their personal tips and 'hacks' for using your product. In fact, Everyone Social suggests that more than half of consumers (50%) wish that brands would tell them what type of content to create and share. [28]

This allows for a deliberate approach to User generated Content (UGC). UGC is becoming increasingly important

---

[28] https://everyonesocial.com/blog/user-generated-content-statistics/)

for content creation and here are three compelling reasons why:

1. 92% of consumers turn to people they know for referrals above any other source. [29]
2. 84% of consumers say they trust peer recommendations above all other sources of advertising. [30]
3. 79% of people say UGC highly impacts their purchasing decisions. [31]

As a matter of course, for 15 minutes everyday, search your brand on Facebook, Twitter, LinkedIn, TikTok and Reddit (setting up Google Alerts will help you stay on top of this plus whenever you are mentioned in other articles across the web). Reply to and interact with any mentions and if appropriate, ask for permission to re-share.

---

[29] pages.tapinfluence.com/hs-fs/hub/256900/file-2517585402-pdf/Influencers_vs._Advocates_-_Whats_the_Difference_eBook_Final_v2.pdf)

[30] pages.tapinfluence.com/hs-fs/hub/256900/file-2517585402-pdf/Influencers_vs._Advocates_-_Whats_the_Difference_eBook_Final_v2.pdf

[31] https://everyonesocial.com/blog/user-generated-content-statistics/

In time, we should aim for 80% of content to be user-generated, with 20% created by our teams. This ambition might seem lofty, but with the increasingly influential power of social media and the fact that 92% of consumers turn to others for product recommendations it's a fact that we can't ignore.

It's my view that over time the results of a marketing team will be driven by how good they are at inspiring others and *curating* others content rather than just how good they are at *creating* it.

We'll be covering the power of influence and advocacy in the next few chapters, but let's now go onto the final element of 'inspired' creativity, 'entertainment' value content.

In creating inspired entertainment content, this is where following meme accounts can be really useful. Accounts like Lad Bible or The Archbishop of Banterbury, for example. Also, spending five minutes per morning looking at what's trending on Twitter and TikTok will give you the opportunity to jump on any trends you feel are appropriate, without having to spend your day glued to social media channels.

When we see things that are trending, we can make decisions around the content that we should use. In addition, follow those brand accounts that typically jump on trends early, like Innocent, Deliveroo, McDonalds or Wendys which will give you the insight into what's blowing up right now. If you follow those brands, you'll notice that they are often commenting on the content that's trending, rather than just doing their own take on it, and some of these comments get thousands of likes and provide incredible exposure for the brand.

But, you also might want to contribute to these trends, TikTok and Instagram Reels are leaning in on making content go viral with Duets and Remixes, enabling you to evolve a meme or trend with your own take.

A good example of jumping on the back of trends is Deliveroo joining in with the Twitter Audio Spaces sensation that was 'Sing your Dialect' — an open karaoke session which invited people across the world to sing a song in their local dialect. It blew up and has now become a regular 'thing' with big names such as singer Shakira, England footballer Declan Rice and WWE star John Cena getting involved.

With over 50,000 viewers at any one time, trends like this provide brands with immediate exposure to a captive audience.

Another good example of brand involvement in trending content was the Weetabix and Beans collaboration. This surprising collaboration sparked social media outrage and many brands, from KFC to the US Embassy jumped in to have their say. [32] The conversations that happened between brands in this particular example brought a truly human element to these organisations, an essential component to feeling a connection with a brand.

This is the power of trends, whilst we can't build a strategy around these fleeting moments, this is the point where social media is at its most powerful, taking over international narratives and capturing imaginations. These are golden opportunities for brands.

Any trending moment that happens, be it the Superbowl, the Oscars just a particular National Day (of which there is one for pretty much anything), are opportunities for our brands to jump in and have our say.

---

[32] https://www.bbc.co.uk/food/articles/controversial_breakfast_tweet

As a simple example, from a small business perspective at ContentCal, for 'National Dog Day', we got every member of the team to take a picture with their pup. We posted a carousel of a collection of these pictures across all of our social channels and it was little surprise that it became one of the best performing posts of the year.

Business is human and social media is called 'social' for a reason. People care about people, not brands.

Empowered with our creative inspiration, let's now focus on community.

CUSTOMER
CONTEXT
CREATIVITY
COMMUNITY
CHANNELS
CALCULATION

CHAPTER 13
BUILDING TRUST.
THE IMPORTANCE OF EMPLOYEE
ADVOCACY

Social media is forcing us to rethink how we, as B2B's approach marketing. Increasingly, we're seeing the personalities within business shine brighter than the brands themselves. Take Steven Bartlett [33], formerly of Social Chain. His personal brand was stronger than the business. Similarly, look at Dave Gerhardt [34], formerly of business live-chat provider, Drift. It's the same situation. Also, look at what Carrie Rose[35] is doing and how she's leading the growth of her marketing agency, Rise at Seven through her personal brand.

This approach is not just for CEO's either. Rise at Seven's approach to marketing is social-first and orientated around giving the team a voice. This is not just about providing equal opportunities either, showcasing the personalities within a business generates human connection, increases the reach of the content (as opposed to sharing content only from the branded channels) and showcases the expertise within the business. Rise at Seven's meteoric rise has all been driven through word of mouth that was made possible through understanding the 'right' way to approach social media.

---

[33] https://www.linkedin.com/in/stevenbartlett-123/

[34] https://www.linkedin.com/in/davegerhardt/

[35] https://www.linkedin.com/in/carrieroseballoch/

This approach is known as 'employee advocacy'.

It's well known that B2B decision-makers use thought leadership to vet a company's capabilities. 59% agree that an organization's thought leadership is a more trustworthy source for assessing a company's capabilities than the company's marketing material.[36] In addition, 79% businesses report more online visibility after the implementation of a formal employee advocacy program, and 65% reported increased brand recognition.[37] Most telling of all, is that content shared by employees receives 8x more engagement than content shared by brand channels.[38]

Despite some clear evidence, B2B's have been incredibly slow to realise this opportunity. However, at a macro level, the tides are beginning to turn.

A recent Edelman 'Trust Barometer' report highlighted a clear shift in trust towards 'My CEO' and Co-workers.

---

[36] https://www.edelman.com/research/2020-b2b-thought-leadership-impact-study

[37] www.hingemarketing.com/uploads/hinge-research-employee-advocacy.pdf

[38] www.socialmediatoday.com/content/employee-advocate-mobilize-your-team-share-your-brand-content

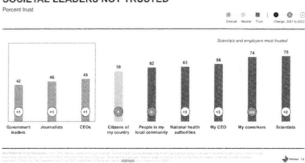

SOCIETAL LEADERS NOT TRUSTED
Percent trust

As trust in governments continues to trend downwards, employees and buyers are looking elsewhere for sources of trusted information. Trust in "My CEO" increased 3 percentage points year-on-year and co-workers remained the second highest most trusted source. As Bob Burg originally wrote in his book "Endless Referrals"; people do business with, and refer business to people they know, like, and trust.

An organisation's beliefs and values has a key part to play in trust-building. As we said at the start of the book, starting with 'why' and understanding your purpose is essential, not just for marketing, but for all human interactions with a business.

ALL STAKEHOLDERS HOLD BUSINESS ACCOUNTABLE

58%
Will buy or advocate for brands based on their beliefs and values

60%
Will choose a place to work based on their beliefs and values

64%
Will invest based on their beliefs and values

According to Edelman's report, 58% of people will buy or advocate for brands based on the organisation's beliefs and values. These values will underpin buying decisions, hence demonstrating these values, beliefs and ambitions through your employee base becomes an essential part of winning hearts and minds.

Take this simple example from Watford Football Club. This chart tracks their club level YouTube subscribers in comparison to their goalkeeper, Ben Foster's.[39]

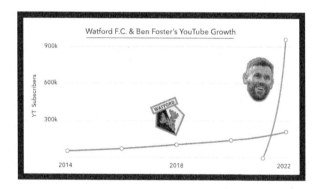

Watford F.C. & Ben Foster's YouTube Growth

---

[39] https://marketingexamples.com/brand/personal

Simply put, people care more about the person than they do about the brand.

As Dave Gerhardt says,

Dave Gerhardt @davegerhardt · Apr 28, 2020
Don't build a marketing team.

Build a media company for your niche.

Based on this, it's my prediction that the future of B2B social media will be driven by personal brands and subject matter experts that evangelise their category. That doesn't mean we all need to shut down our company pages, but when we're creating content, we need to be thinking broader than just our branded channels.

It's not just a case of executing in a contemporary way that matches how influence actually happens, employee advocacy makes rational sense too. Calling on the collective of your employee bases' following allows brands to increase the reach of their content by an order of magnitude.

Despite the clear and obvious benefits of employee advocacy, there have typically been three elements that have held businesses back from realising its potential.

- **Fear** - Employees are worried about sharing their view and how they will be perceived.
- **Creativity** - Employees are often unsure what to post
- **Time** - Employees have a day job to do, which will always take precedence.

These barriers are all solvable through the following steps.

To address the fear of perception, we should return back to our themes that we created in the previous step.

- Ideation
- Creation
- Process and Workflow
- Collaboration
- Publishing
- Analytics
- News
- How-to

These themes will help employees' focus their content on the topics that fit the business and, as we already know from our research, are areas of most value for our audience.

These themes also help steer creativity. Each individual should aim to post three times per week, and for each of these days there should be a different theme. For example, Monday's post could be about 'process and workflow', Wednesday's could be on 'collaboration' and Friday's could be a 'How to'. This takes the guesswork and cognitive load out of content creation.

In addition, I would recommend having a 'bank' of content that employees can access that is organised by these themes, enabling these employees to access this content to simply re-use and share on their channels. (There are many tools available that you can do this with, or just keep a well-organised Google Drive). This also works in reverse too, if you encourage your employees to share content suggestions, like we mentioned in the previous chapter, this allows the marketing team to finesse that content and make it available for employees to use.

Also, an easy way for employees to begin is simply by re-sharing content from the company page or from other employees or influential people they follow. This is not the most effective approach, as original content performs better, but it's a start.

There are two other approaches that also solve the creativity challenge, along with the challenge of time. Firstly, your employees might not want to create content themselves, but still like the idea of building their following and personal brands. In this instance you could create the content on behalf of these employees, send it to them for approval (using an approval tool like ContentCal), which would allow them to add some personalisation if they wanted to and then it's just a case of them tapping 'approve' and the content will be published to their social profile automatically.

Or, in the other scenario, an employee might not want to put their personal spin or approval on the content and is just happy with content regularly being published to their profile. In this case you can just use a social media scheduling tool to push out your content to multiple employees personal profiles, increasing both your reach and impact of your content.

One example of a business that has leaned in on employee advocacy is Colt Technologies.

Social Media Manager, Jake Potter suggests these tips for any organisation embarking on an employee advocacy program.

- **Make it easy**: people won't engage if the program is complex.
- **Allow message amendment:** social messages you provide for advocacy should be advisable, so people can edit them to make it sound more personal.
- **Don't be the social media police:** you don't have the time to monitor social media for all of your employees, and you'll disengage participants if you micromanage the process. Keep an eye out for huge mistakes or non-external facing comments, but otherwise, let it go.

On a personal note, having a 'face' of ContentCal, was one of the best decisions we made in terms of driving our social media growth. It created a truly personal connection with an audience, follower growth happened much quicker, content reached more people (as we all know personal profiles out perform company pages, particularly on LinkedIn), it built trust and humanised our brand and as such, it became a competitive differentiator.

Now that we've understood the impact of internal influence, let's now look at how we leverage influence and advocacy externally.

CUSTOMER
CONTEXT
CREATIVITY
COMMUNITY
CHANNELS
CALCULATION

CHAPTER 14
CREATORS AND INFLUENCERS. BUILDING TRUST THROUGH AFFILIATION

Over the last seven years 'Influencer marketing' has grown by 854% and as of 2022, is estimated to be worth $16.4 billion [40]

But what is 'Influencer marketing'?
Whilst Influencer marketing might be a fairly recent term, it's actually nothing new.

---

[40] https://influencermarketinghub.com/influencer-marketing-statistics/

In essence, it involves brands working with individuals that have a large audience and are admired by the audience the brand wants to target. Even back in 1984, Nike signed a $2.5m deal with Michael Jordan and sold £70m worth of trainers in the first year. It just wasn't called 'influencer marketing' then.

But what has changed is that those with 'influence' are no longer just sports or film stars, social media has created a platform for personalities to flourish and audiences to become increasingly fragmented.

There are now approximately 18m Instagram accounts with over 100,000 followers[41] and this presents marketers and brands with an incredible opportunity.

For brands, working with influencers is a way to shortcut trust. As we've already mentioned, 'trust' is at the foundation of buying decisions and as we also shared earlier, 92% of consumers turn to people they know for referrals above any other source and again, for most buyers, **the best product is the one they know.**

---

[41] https://mention.com/en/reports/instagram/followers/#2

As social media ads become increasingly expensive and as we enter the cookie-less age where targeting the right users with our ads will continue to be more challenging, this will serve to make influencer marketing increasingly appealing for marketers.

As influencer marketing matures, we're now seeing new challenges and new opportunities. We're still early on into the regulation of the social media influencer industry, where there is growing pressure for transparency and for influencers to clearly state that their content is a paid promotion, rather than just adding #ad in the caption.

The new opportunities that are emerging are as a result of the meteoric rise of social media. Marketers are starting to realise that in terms of overall follower numbers, bigger might not always mean better. As influencer marketing evolves, the focus is, rightly, turning to audience quality.

We're now seeing terms like 'nano' and 'micro' influencers become part of the industry's narrative. According to MediaKix, nano-influencers have up to 10,000 followers, micro-influencers are defined as accounts with anywhere from 10,000-50,000 followers and macro-influencers as accounts with 500,000-1 million followers. It's at the nano and micro levels where I believe for most brands the real opportunity is.

At these smaller levels, the audience is often very focussed on a specific niche as opposed to the typically more general interest of the followers of macro influencers. It means more work for brands in building relationships with more influencers, but it adds more diversity to the brand voice along with more specific content that's targeted at a certain audience. For B2B's this is especially important. Companies like IBM are working with AI and data science influencers and whilst it might be a stretch to think they'll have the same reach as Kylie Jenner, the audience that are consuming such focussed content is likely to be their perfect target.

This fragmentation of influence has caused another, and possibly even more interesting macro shift. The rise of the 'creator economy' has been well documented and is tangentially linked to the growth in the 'gig' and 'passion' economy. In each case, it's linked to society's desire to gain more control of their livelihoods and lead the life they desire.

We can see the creator economy's growth all around us; from the growth of Esty and Not on the High Street to the growth of subscription platforms like Patreon, Substack and OnlyFans. As a society we've never has so much access and opportunity to build businesses from our bedrooms.

Covid has accelerated this growth and now people are quitting their jobs and pursuing new careers at unprecedented rates. According to the Bureau of Labor Statistics (BLS), the "quits rate" in the U.S. reached an all-time high, with four million people quitting their jobs in April 2021 alone — in a trend that's now being called the 'The great resignation'.

Many participants in the creator economy are now turning to social media to build their audiences and create the life they desire.

More than 50 million people worldwide consider themselves to be creators and they are now part of a $100bn industry.[42] Of these, 46.7 million think of themselves as amateurs, with two million-plus considering themselves to be professional creators, earning enough from their passion to consider it their full-time income.

---

[42] https://www.economist.com/the-world-ahead/2021/11/08/li-jin-on-the-future-of-the-creator-economy

So what's the key differences between content creators and influencers? According to Neil Patel, [43] content creators are more focused on creating and publishing content to support their own personal endeavour, while influencers are more focused on building an audience and promoting brands. They also operate differently. Content creators create original content for sharing knowledge or building a personal brand, while influencers (particularly macro and mega influencers) post sponsored content for money and popularity.

Whether someone would class themselves as a creator or an influencer, one thing is clear, these already impressive numbers are only going one way. Social media platforms are currently engaged in a war for talent, offering increasingly tantalising financial incentives to create content on their platform. For example, we've seen the $100m YouTube fund for creators to create short-form video content, Snapchat did the same with their $100m Spotlight find and Meta have earmarked $1bn for creators.

Some find this hard to believe: giving free money to creators just for creating content on the platform, can that be right? Yes, and it's actually a bargain for the platforms.

---

43 https://neilpatel.com/blog/creator-vs-influencer/

Social platforms live and die by their monthly active audience — getting the best creators means getting the best content, creators bring the audience and the content keeps them consuming, and the more consumption of content there is, the more social platforms make money. The formula is simple: If you get the influencers, you will likely get the eyeballs, and if you get the eyeballs, you get the advertisers and their dollars.

The upshot of all of this is that Creators and influencers solve two of marketers' greatest challenges: Relevance and Reach.

Relevance

Relevance is achieved by keeping pace with culture. The pace of change in culture has arguably never been as rapid as it is right now; we just need to look at how 2020 played out to see a stark reminder of that. Working in collaboration with others that are better placed to advise and create content on behalf of a brand in light of cultural moments will help ensure that if you do elect to have a voice in a certain moment, you have the right means of delivering that message. Relevance is not just about cultural moments either, it's about finding authentic, respected and trusted voices to represent your brand.

Reach

47% of internet users now use ad blockers[44] and Apple's iOS 14.5 privacy update has resulted in 96% of users opting out of Facebook tracking their usage behaviours[45] and resulted in a $10bn loss for Facebook.[46] Against this backdrop of severely impacted ad reach and targeting capability, marketers are turning to influencers and creators who represent their target audience to create a diverse range of content that they can use to target consumers with personalised content.

Collaborating with creators and influencers also helps increase reach across more platforms. Often brands major on a few select social platforms, and rather then thinking you need to create an audience on TikTok or Snapchat, for example; you can find the right influencer or creator to work with to open up your brand to an audience on a new platform.

[44] https://www.forbes.com/sites/forbescommunicationscouncil/2020/08/06/how-to-tackle-the-rising-cost-of-ad-blocking/?sh=4a08d71368d7)

[45] https://arstechnica.com/gadgets/2021/05/96-of-us-users-opt-out-of-app-tracking-in-ios-14-5-analytics-find/

[46] https://www.cnbc.com/2022/02/02/facebook-says-apple-ios-privacy-change-will-cost-10-billion-this-year.html

In terms of platforms, whilst instagram is the preferred platform for most influencers, TikTok, Twitch, Snapchat and YouTube are becoming increasingly popular.[47]

Collaborating with influential people outside of your business doesn't always mean paying for the privilege. You can find influencers and creators using tools like www.hypeauditor.com. This will help you see who has influence in your category along with their audience size and their audience quality score.

How you will end up collaborating with these individuals will vary, but the best thing you can do in every situation is seek out advocacy. My personal recommendation is to only work with those that truly care about what you're doing.

This means investing the time in building the relationship with these individuals, getting to know their ambitions and helping them understand your mission. For me, advocacy is at the core of every successful relationship, if the influencer truly cares about what you're doing then content creation will be so much easier for them, their endorsement will be genuine and even when they are not being paid, they will still recommend you.

---

[47] https://influencermarketinghub.com/influencer-marketing-statistics/)

Developing these relationships with creators and influencers also requires a creative approach to commercials. Those that have spent time building an audience will not share content they do not believe in (if they are happy to, that's a red flag) and as a result, it's not always a case of paying money for a post in a transactional way. In fact, many creators and influencers want long term partnerships, and in our experience they result in the most successful relationships.

This means you might need to get more creative with the value exchange. It might be straight payment, or it might be providing free access to your product or access to something else that's of value to them (maybe time with your CEO). Or, the value exchange might be a retained monthly payment or discounts you can offer to their community. The key is to ask at the beginning of every partnership; 'what would a successful partnership look like to you?'

Once you've found the right individuals(s) to work with and have figured out the right value exchange, now we need to consider the activity. It might be a social media post, video or story or it could be a contribution to a blog, a review of your product, or maybe you'd like to interview them on your podcast or webinar.

Creating content with others can take longer, but is likely to be more successful due to the varied perspectives it includes, helping you increase both the relevance and reach of your content.

Collaboration is key to social media success and in the final chapter on 'community', we're going to empower collaboration through a community.

CUSTOMER
CONTEXT
CREATIVITY
COMMUNITY
CHANNELS
CALCULATION

CHAPTER 15
THE POWER OF COMMUNITY.
CREATING TRUST THROUGH
CONNECTION

If you've not started already, the most valuable thing your marketing team could do this year is create a community. A thriving community can become a company's most valuable asset, rich with advocacy, trust and market insight.

In a world full of commoditised products, a brands'
community can be the differentiator.

Businesses are beginning to realise that they need to 'own'
their communities and are realising that 'community'
means more than just a social media follower count. A
community is defined by who you choose to prioritise
with your content — focussing on the interests of the
audience above the interests of the business.

As decision-making becomes increasingly decentralised,
and business software & services decision making flows to
the end-user, the trust and brand connection that can be
facilitated at scale through a community can become a
businesses biggest driver of organic growth. As such, a
new term has been coined; 'Community-Led Growth'

In a B2B setting, there are typically two types of
communities:

- Product-based — These communities are focused
  on discussing and learning about a specific
  product, like Salesforce Trailblazers, or the Notion
  community we shared earlier.

- Category-based— These communities are all about levelling-up a discipline and connecting with other practitioners, like The Hub for Social Media Manager.[48]

Product-based community

For many B2B's, having a community of individuals who care enough about your product to join a community to discuss their usage and share their experiences with others is the ultimate goal. Although it might seem a stretch to think that customers will want to spend their own time talking about how they use your product, in my personal experience at ContentCal however, I've been incredibly surprised to see customers' willingness to do this. In retrospect, I should not have been surprised, as fundamentally as humans, we all desire to be a part of something.

To this end, even if your business is still at an early stage, I'd recommend setting up a community for your existing customers, even if there are just a handful to begin with. Don't expect immediate results, but over time it will grow and in a year or so, you'll be very glad you did.

---

[48] https://www.facebook.com/groups/smmhub/about/

As we've discussed over the course of this book, there is no substitute for being close to customers. These communities will help fuel your product development and finesse your marketing narratives whilst becoming an in-built word or mouth engine for your business. But remember, the community is about others, not your brand.

Or, you might be in the fortunate position that Notion found themselves in. As we shared earlier, Notion noticed that there was a lot of conversation online about their product and even blogs have already been set up by individuals to share how they use Notion. If you find yourself in this position, you'll be on for a fast-start. You can recruit existing advocates to run your community and create a place to centralise all of the existing conversation around your brand.

Category-based community

Whilst a product-based community is a wonderful way to help existing customers feel a sense of belonging whilst empowering product development insights along with loyalty and advocacy, it won't help you reach new audiences in the short term.

This is where category-based communities come in. Category-based communities are less intrinsically linked to a brand and are focussed on helping those that join to increase their skills and learning around a certain subject. Category-based communities also allow you to get granular with targeting your buyer persona. The more niche and specific your community, the better. This was also something we learned through failure at ContentCal - we wanted our category-based community to be a 'catch-all' for content marketers and in hindsight this was too broad.

People want to feel part of a tribe, a safe-space for like minded individuals to ask questions and learn from those that are in a similar position. This is when magic happens within a community, when you get your targeting and topic correct, the community becomes self-perpetuating with the community members asking and answering questions and sharing the community with others, relying less on the group owner to be the content creator, just the moderator.

Two example groups that has done this particularly well are Matt Navarra's Social Media Geek Out Facebook group [49] which targets the pro-level social media manager with latest trends and news, and The Hub for Social Media

---

[49] https://www.facebook.com/groups/socialgeekout/about/

Managers that we touched on earlier, which focuses on freelance social media managers and small social media agencies. Over 90% of conversation in these groups comes from the community. When you nail the target audience, you bake in a degree of natural virality. It's of value to the group members to share the group with others as the more people are part of the group, the more rich, interesting and diverse the insights are.

It's also worthwhile noting that whilst these communities should not be seen as a channel for promotional content, building a community opens up a brand new channel for you to share your creative content that adds value to and is perfectly aligned to your target audience.

Before we start creating our own community, there are some questions we should ask ourselves:

- Who is in our community and why are they here? Who is not in the community?
- What value will we create for the community?
- What value will the members provide each other?
- (If we are building a product-focussed community) How will we listen, talk to, and be directed by our customers?

- How and where will we deliver insights from these conversations to the rest of the company?
- How will we incentivise, recognise, and reward participation in the community?
- Who will run the community?
- How will we maintain growth?

Community can be your businesses' superpower, but whether you're building a product-based or category-based community, it takes time and it needs space to breathe free from KPI's and micro analysis.

There is, however, a way to leverage the impact of community-based marketing to drive short term results.

We've already discussed the creation of an 'owned' community, the process of creating your own community to engage more deeply with your customers or your target audience. But, we can also consider 'non-owned' communities and how we collaborate with other communities to reach new audiences.

Working with non-owned communities

Whilst I consider this community strategy as an addition to the creation of your 'owned' communities, this approach can yield more short-term results. To begin with, search Facebook for groups related to your category and do the same on other community-orientated platforms like Twitter, Reddit and Discord. Look for where the conversation is happening around your category (for ContentCal it was mostly Facebook Groups) and join these groups to get a feel for the types of conversations that are happening around your category.

The next step is to get involved with these conversations, adding value by answering questions, but ensuring that you don't use this as an opportunity for self-promotion. (Many groups' rules prevent link sharing). Once you've created a list of applicable groups and communities and have got a feel for the level of interaction in these groups, the next step is to reach out to the group owner to strike up a conversation.

We want to approach these conversations with long-term partnership and a mutual value exchange in mind, not a mindset of 'I want to promote my content to your audience'.

It was in these approaches that arguably we saw the biggest success from ContentCal's community strategy. Here are three examples of how we leveraged 'non-owned' communities to drive our growth.

The Marketing Meetup

From searching marketing communities in the UK online I noticed a community called 'The Marketing Meetup'. This community revolved around physical meetups along with a Facebook Group. The community is run by two truly wonderful human; Joe Glover and James Sandbrook. These two individuals are no stranger to being pitched by marketing software companies, so I decided to take an approach which led with interest and gratitude first, as opposed to treating them as a media channel (which seems to be the typical MO of many B2B's).

I attended one of their London meetings to get a flavour of the community and get a feel for the types of conversation that was happening amongst community members. It was a fantastic way to understand whether this community was right for us and also what we would need to do for this community to ensure we add value as a partner.

It was this approach that allowed us to have a much more constructive partnership conversation when I approached

James at the end of the event. Whenever you're wanting to create a new partnership it's always helpful to have an idea in mind of what you can bring to the table to benefit your partner first. Long story short, the Marketing Meetup team and ContentCal became very good friends, embarking on a long term relationship which included a financial exchange but more importantly, included us producing content in partnership with them, for example;

- Research reports (communities are incredible for generating insights)
- Monthly live social media training for community members
- Speaking
- Blogs
- Podcast

As the Marketing Meetup grew, especially throughout the pandemic, the events went online and community members ballooned, ContentCal has continued to permeate an ever increasing audience.

Over time, familiarity of ContentCal grew and because community members typically ask other community members what tools and products are using, as soon as someone starts to recommend ContentCal, the fire of word-of-mouth builds and trust in your product and your brand starts to permeate throughout the community.

The Marketing Meetup still remains one of the best sources of new business for ContentCal, it truly is sustainable in nature, as more people continue to join an ever-growing community become aware of your brand and as your reputation grows off the back of the content you create, trust in your brand grows, as does word of mouth.

Whilst The Marketing Meetup gave us coverage for marketers operating in small business, we also wanted to work with a community that indexed highly on social media managers. For this reason, we chose to work with Matt Navarra as part of The Social Media Geek Out Facebook Group. Matt's Facebook community gave us access to professional social media managers. With Matt we partnered on a series of webinars creating a platform for education for both Matt's and ContentCal's audiences, and allowed promotion of these webinars to a wider audience.

As most of Matt's content is written, it made sense to bring his expertise to life with a live webinar. Over the course of the partnership, ContentCal was subtly and slowly introduced, building trust throughout his community. Three years after beginning our work together, ContentCal is still continually referenced and recommended within group community chats and Matt remains a fantastic partner for the brand.

In this Final example, we worked with The Hub for Social Media Managers. This community is intensely focused on what was our initial buyer persona of small agencies and social media freelancers. This community is a free community that facilitates the growth of the organisers' business and as a result, they need to be very mindful of working with any other businesses as it goes against their strategy for their group. Essentially they have built their community as a growth engine for their training business, so working with others and using their community to benefit other businesses is not in absolute alignment with their business model. (You'll find this with many communities you come across.) Often they've been set up to serve the needs of a bigger business, so that means we need to be mindful of the value we can bring to the table that will benefit their community.

In the case of the Hub for Social Media Managers, the value we offered was educational content, primarily focused on social media analytics. Analytics was a particular area where they had discovered their audience were struggling and in this scenario we simply represented a gap in expertise for the organisers. Here we added immediate value by providing our expertise free of charge. We also went even further by providing free access to our product to the owners of the group to show a long-term commitment, along with providing a discount for any group members. We had the interests of the community at heart and it opened up one of the most valuable non-paid, organic initiatives we created.

These three communities (along with many others) have fuelled our organic growth engine at ContentCal and continue to do so. These relationships took time to build, like most good relationships do, but they provide value in excess of any financial investment and contribute to create a defensible and differentiated go-to-market strategy.

As you'll have been able to see so far, community impacts each stage of the marketing funnel from awareness and consideration to loyalty and advocacy.

In fact, We Are Social cites word-of-mouth referrals as the 3rd highest source of brand discovery, behind search engines and TV ads.

Community platforms

Creating or becoming part of a community takes time and that requires the right growth mindset that is not fixated on immediate results. For those that are willing, there is incredible opportunity awaiting brands who leverage community-based marketing.

Where you create your group and how you incentivise and support members are critical pieces to consider. Platform-wise, generally-speaking, you have three routes:

- Social media-based community
    - Example: Facebook Groups, Instagram, Twitter, Discord or Reddit
    - Pro: Quicker growth as users are already native to these platforms
    - Con: Lack of ownership and control

- Community platform
    - Example: Mighty Networks or Guild
    - Pro: More control, more organisation and better content discovery for those on the platform

- ○   Con: Slower growth as users are required to frequent a new platform

- • Own platform
  - ○   Example: Creating a community element on your own website
  - ○   Pro: The best control and easiest discovery outside social media
  - ○   Con: Time to market

In all cases, we need to think of community-based marketing as 'value creation' rather than 'value capture'. Community is at the heart of a business strategy, and is not just a marketing channel. As such we need to give it the space for conversations to happen without the pressure of sales targets and KPIs. In other words, you can't force a flower to grow, but you can create the ideal environment for its growth.

This means that community building needs to be a core business competency: one with the team, budgets, tooling, and support from the leadership team. When companies create more value than they capture, people learn new things, meet new people, and discover new opportunities — all of which act as a force multiplier for your business.

Before we move on from community, there is one final shift that has the potential to unlock even more value in community creation.

Communities and 'Creator Coins'

We're going to cover Web 3.0 in the next chapter, but in short, Web 3.0 is changing the power dynamic of the internet. In Web 2.0 where all of the power is held by the platforms (Facebook etc.), Web3 changes this and shifts the power to the content creators and provides an infrastructure to align contribution with financial reward.

One Web3-based approach we've begun to see communities taking is through the creation of 'creator coins'.

Though creator coins (aka social tokens) are in their nascent stage, they are quickly becoming a powerful tool that, in time, every community will want to leverage. Creator Coins give community members an actual stake in the success of the community.

Now, imagine the potential of growing a community by using creator coins, it elevates your audience's role in the community, since they have a currency, they're more likely to get and stay involved in the community.

Like most currency economies, people can buy, hold, and sell your coins. But unlike most, they also can receive benefits unique to your community. You get to decide what they get.

To demonstrate some early examples of creator coins in action, here's a couple of examples:

Brian Clark created $MOVE coin. The founder of Copyblogger, Brian also publishes Further, a personal growth newsletter, and launched Unemployable, an educational community for solopreneurs.

He has built a thriving Discord community talking creator coins and NFTs for coin holders with at least $15 USD in $MOVE coins. This group also receives 10% off training and events. Community members who increase their investment to $120 USD of $MOVE gain VIP access to exclusive small group coaching and 50% off training and other events.

The Tilt community of content marketers also has its own coin. While they can be purchased, readers and contributors also can earn them for referring new subscribers, contributing guest blog posts, and more. As founder Joe Pulizzi explains:

"At The Tilt, we believe that the audience and community we are working to build should also benefit financially. These are the early days, but social tokens and creator coins are a start. Web 3.0 is all about audience collectives, and we need to be prepared for this."

Creator coins are beginning to align the interests of business and community members and incentives desired behaviours. For example, if you want your community members to share the word about your community, giving them a financial stake and upside in doing so makes perfect sense.

As we go into the final two steps of the SOCIAL 3.0 Framework, let's recap on where we've got to so far.

1. **Persona and problem space.** We identified our minimum viable audience and identified the challenges they face

2. **Value proposition.** We built on our hypothesis of the problem statement and have got clear on our purpose (our 'why')

3. **Customer Discovery.** We embarked on marketing research through quantitative analysis and with real-life customer conversation to validate our value proposition

4. **Story.** We took our research and resulting learnings to craft a story that speaks the language of our audience,

5. **Objective.** Before we started creating any content, we got clarity about what we wanted to achieve

6. **Creativity.** We've unlocked content creation through qualitative, quantitative and inspired creativity.

7. **Community.** We've understood the importance of delivering this creativity to market in a community-led way through internal advocacy, influencers and communities

We're now going to create a plan for how we'll bring our creative ideas to life through communities and social channels.

CUSTOMER
CONTEXT
CREATIVITY
COMMUNITY
CHANNELS
CALCULATION

CHAPTER 16
OWNED MEDIA.
HOW TO MAXIMISE LEVERAGE OF YOUR 'OWNED' CHANNELS AND THE IMPACT OF WEB 3.0

In this chapter, we'll be focussing on both the core and emerging social media channels that we can leverage to scale the distribution of our content.

To begin, let's go back to our work in the creative process and give ourselves a reminder of the content 'themes' and formats that we are working to;

- Ideation
- Creation
- Process and Workflow
- Collaboration
- Publishing
- Analytics
- News
- How-to

With our high-level content strategy in place, it's now time to take our themes and formats and build these into a tactical plan.

Core channels

Before we can build this tactical plan however, we need to think about all of the different opportunities the social platforms present us with. It's not just different platforms we need to consider, it's the different post formats on these platforms we need to consider too. To give you a feel for the range of choice we have at our disposal, this (non-exhaustive) list below gives you a feel.

Publishing Channels & Formats							
Facebook	Image	Carousel	Video	Live	Story	Group	
Twitter	Image	Carousel	Video	Live	Audio Space		
LinkedIn	Image	Carousel	Video	Live	Personal Profiles		
Instagram	Image	Carousel	Video	Live	Story	Reel	Personal Profiles
TikTok	Video	Live	Personal Profiles				
Snapchat	Story	Video					
Pinterest	Image	Carousel	Video	Live	Story		
Google My Business	Image						
YouTube	Video	Live	Shorts				
Communities	Facebook	Reddit	Quora	Discord			

If this seems daunting, it need not be. We're going to simplify and make sense of this over the course of this chapter.

The importance of a 'multi-channel' approach.

According to Data Reportal,[50] the average number of social media accounts an individual has is 7.5. In addition, across all of the major platforms, less than 1% of users are

---

[50] https://datareportal.com/reports/digital-2022-global-overview-report

unique to the platform, meaning that if we want to reach our target audience, we need to be publishing content across more channels than ever before.

It used to be that a typical approach to B2B social media would be to publish content to Twitter and LinkedIn only. But when you consider that over 83% of LinkedIn users are also on Instagram, do we really want to miss that opportunity?

The shifting sands of social

Thinking about a multi-channel approach is also essential to help us maximise the reach of our content. It's no secret that from an organic (non-paid) social media perspective we are fighting ever decreasing reach. Naturally, with diminishing reach comes a reduction in engagement. As an example, the average engagement rate on Facebook is now a lowly 0.07%.[51]

This means that we need to change our previously held views about which channels we should leverage for our business. Demographics across social platforms are constantly changing, to a point that over 50's now

---

[51] https://datareportal.com/reports/digital-2022-global-overview-report

outnumber social media users that are 13-19 years old. Social media connects 58% of the world population and it's our job to be open-minded about the platforms, formats and approaches that give us the best opportunity to unlock its potential.

Message and Formats > Channel

Personally, I have never subscribed to the notion that you need to speak to people in different ways on different platforms. The only time that approach makes some sense is if you are targeting a totally different audience on separate platforms. Typically however, this approach shows a lack of focus on a core audience and as a result will struggle for growth. If you've completed the steps of the SOCIAL 3.0 framework correctly, you will have truly understood the emotional drivers of your minimum viable audience and can tell a story that resonates with them.

The story always comes before the channel. Just because someone opened their Instagram rather than their LinkedIn, doesn't mean they've suddenly become a different person with different motivations. If we've got the message right, the channel is the easy part.

As one of my favourite B2B marketers, Louis Grenier says; *'New tool? New channel? New whatever? No problem. I can learn about it and apply the same principles.'*

The same logic applies to formats. The earlier showed the plethora of social media channels and formats. At first glance, it might seem that the options seem overwhelming, but if you start to break it down, it's not actually that complex.

	Facebook	Instagram	Twitter	Linked In	Tik Tok	Snapchat	Pinterest	You Tube
Short Form Video	X	X	X	X	X	X	X	X
Live	X	X	X	X	X		X	X
Image	X	X	X	X			X	
Carousel	X	X	X	X			X	
Story	X	X				X	X	
Long Form Video	X	X						X
Audio	X		X					
Duets/ Remixing		X			X			
Collabs		X			X			

Essentially, there are nine different formats of content we can create across all of the social media platforms. If you look at the core content formats offered by each social platform, and organise it by popularity, five key trends begin to emerge;

1. Short-form video

I'm classing 'short-form' here as videos under 3 minutes in length. This format has become ubiquitous across platforms, and is the key focus area for TikTok, Snapchat, Instagram, Facebook and YouTube. The social platforms are locked in a war for attention, vying over who can encourage users to spend the most time on their platform. YouTube is currently winning this battle, but is being chased by TikTok, of which the average users spends nearly double the time on compared to Instagram (19.6 hours per month for TikTok vs 11.2 for Instagram.) [52]

This matters a great deal for our organic strategies as the platforms need to encourage more engagement on short-form video content to drive up view time and engagement and for us as brands and marketers, that means we get a boost in organic reach.

---

[52] https://datareportal.com/reports/digital-2022-global-overview-report

2. Live-streaming.

Live-streaming is the content format that is responsible for the growth in time spent on the top 5 social networks.[53] It's also reported that Facebook live videos generate 6X more interactions than regular videos.[54] This means that live streaming gives us an opportunity to circumvent the reduction in reach and engagement that we get through our typical feed posts

3. Carousels

Carousels are nothing new, but have nearly triple the engagement rate of single image posts on Instagram[55] and also perform similarly well on Facebook.

Noticing the direction of travel of the social platforms gives us an opportunity to benefit from boosted reach, by leveraging the content formats that the social networks are wanting to increase usage of.

---

[53] https://www.data.ai/en/insights/market-data/evolution-of-social-media-report/

[54] https://truelist.co/blog/live-video-statistics/

[55] https://datareportal.com/reports/digital-2022-global-overview-report

The next two trends to add to the mix are what I'd class as the new standard for how we drive engagement on social media.

4. Duets and Remixing

Duets are a concept popularised by TikTok and revolves around users creating their own 'take' on a piece of content. As an example, a packaging brand could publish a video on TikTok showing their goods packaging process and ask their viewers to film themselves attempting to replicate it. 'Duets' allow users to play the original content alongside their 'take' on the content, creating a 'content pyramid' of user-generated content, which can start a trend and provide you with fantastic content to repurpose. As you can tell from this example, the depth of engagement is much more meaningful than a simple like or comment on a post.

Instagram has taken note of the growth of Duets on TikTok and have come up with their own solution of 'remixing' for their TikTok competitor, Reels.

5. Collabs

The importance of collaboration on social content cannot be overstated. Collaboration is the essential component of every marketing strategy. Collaborating with others on content has a multiplier effect. It makes for better content that factors in different perspectives and allows both parties to reach new audiences. The 'collabs' feature is becoming increasingly popular on social platforms, supported first by TikTok, copied by Instagram and now Twitter.

Thinking of these five trends gives our content plan additional structure and will enable us to maximise the performance of our organic content.

The key here is in thinking 'format-first'

Creating a format-first plan

Themes	Ideate	Create	Process & Workflow	Collab	Publish	Analyse	News	How-to
Formats								
Short Form Video	X							
Live			X					
Image								
Carousel								
Story								
Long Form Video								
Audio								
Duets								
Collabs								
Channels								
Facebook	X		X					
Twitter			X					
Instagram	X		X					
TikTok	X		X					
LinkedIn			X					
Snapchat	X							
Pinterest								
Reddit								
Clubhouse								
YouTube	X		X					

Building on the themes we created in our 'Creativity Triangle' creative process, we can layer on the formats that we believe will be the best vehicle for our content, both in terms of the formats' suitability to convey the message and the opportunity to maximise reach.

In the example on the previous page, we've taken two examples. Firstly, we believe that content related to the theme of 'ideation' will be best served as a short-form video. We can then consider how we re-purpose this short-form content across all of the social platforms that support this format to maximise the reach of this content.

Similarly with the 'Process & Workflow' theme, we might deem that delivering education on this topic through a social live stream is the best format for this content and as such, this gives us the opportunity to distribute this live stream to multiple platforms. (Many tools facilitate broadcasting live streams to multiple social platforms simultaneously, including Zoom)

We would then bring these themes, formats and channels into our content schedule, which might look something like this;

Content Schedule

Schedule					
Day	**Monday**	**Tuesday**	**Wednesday**	**Thursday**	**Friday**
Channel					
Facebook	Ideation - Short Form Video		Process & Workflow - Livestream		Publishing - Carousel
Twitter			Process & Workflow - Livestream		
Instagram	Ideation - Short Form Video		Process & Workflow - Livestream		Publishing - Carousel
TikTok	Ideation - Short Form Video		Process & Workflow - Livestream		
LinkedIn			Process & Workflow - Livestream		Publishing - Carousel

With the core of our content plan set, we now need to consider the multiplying effects that will help amplify our content. We call these 'content multipliers.'

Content multipliers

1. Personal profiles

Personal profiles outperform brand accounts. Not just in terms of reach (any comparative test on LinkedIn, for example will show significantly more reach from your personal profile in comparison to your company page), but also in terms of resonance. According to Social media Today, content shared by employees receives 8x more engagement than content shared by brand channels. We've discussed employee advocacy already, but in your content plan, ensure you consider distribution beyond your brand channels.

2. Audience participation

I hope it's become abundantly clear throughout the course of this book that all of your content needs to be audience-first. Consider audience participation in all of the content you create.

There are number of ways to do this:

- Ask your audience to share their views on a topic

- Ask your audience what content they'd like to see from you

- Ask your audience to tag a friend. (An example here in a ContentCal context would be asking the audience to tag who they think creates great content)

- Lean into 'collabs.' From your work in uncovering influencers in the 'Community' step, who can you create content with that serves mutual benefit for each others' audiences?

- Use polls. Gain valuable insight from your audience and don't forget to create the content that shares the results. This gives users a reason to follow you and return to your content.

- Lean into Duets and Remixes. What content can you create that you can encourage users to try and mimic you?

- Use the 'add yours' sticker on Instagram Stories, encouraging interaction on your content.

- Encourage sharing as much as possible. Ask followers things like what books they are reading, who inspires them, their goals and ambitions. Apply all your learnings from the 'Community' step to your day-to-day social content. If we treat our followers as a community, rather than seeing them as akin to an email subscriber list, we'll see much better results

3. **User Generated Content**

The future of social media will be driven by User Generated Content. By encouraging user participation, you'll begin to gather content from your audience that has the potential to have more impact than the content we can create ourselves.

There's likely already content being shared about your business online already. Search for this content across social platforms and for any content you want to re-share, ask permission from the creator and use this in your content plan.

In addition to the above, you could encourage your audience to share their tips and tricks for how they use your product to complete their task. Even if it's a scrappy video, the fact it's come from a real-life, relatable and genuine user of your product — on social channels, content like this is an order of magnitude more impactful than any highly produced brand video.

Emerging channels

It might seem that the trends of social media and the broader internet are hard to predict, but actually they follow a pretty similar pattern.

Typically it works like this: A trend starters in Asia, gets adopted by US teens, then adults across the western world. B2C brands begin getting involved, then at some point down the track, B2B's wake up.

There are multiple examples of this already: Emojis, video streaming, esports… Emojis are a classic example. First it was big in Japan, then teens. Now we all use it. Then it was baked into Slack and everything else.

If you want to know what B2B communication will look like in 5 years? It's inevitable that livestreaming, virtual goods, NFTs, social tokens, social commerce, the Metaverse and a host of others all eventually end up in the enterprise.

There's a 3-5 year lag, but it definitely happens. TikTok is a great example that's mid-phase. Crossing from Asia into US teens, into adults and now being experimented with at a B2C level.

On that basis, smart companies will build on TikTok. Not to get 'leads' next quarter but to play the long game. There's tremendous upside for B2B companies on TikTok over the next 1-3 years.

We've touched on NFTs and social tokens a couple of times now, so it's about time we dive into Web3 as this is the biggest underlying shift that will impact our content strategy over the next 3-5 years.

Introduction to Web3

Web 2.0, as it's become known, refers to the large, overarching technology platforms that have broken the business model of media.

Think of businesses like Facebook, Apple, Amazon and any big tech platform that have used their scale and distribution to control the relationship between creator and consumer. In the wake of growing distrust and discontent in these platforms a new paradigm is emerging.

A new generation of technologies is emerging with the promise to change the balance of power. If the Web 2.0 era favoured the platforms, the next generation of innovations—collectively known as Web 3.0—is all about tilting the scales of power and ownership toward creators and users.

Referred to by Marc Andressen as 'the original sin of the internet', monetisation was never part of the infrastructure of the Web 2.0 internet. As a result business models were opaque, advertising-based, and dependent on closed-garden networks, which gave an outsized advantage to platforms.

This lack of payment infrastructure is the reason why so much of the internet is monetised via advertising. This meant that users could be monetised frictionlessly and indirectly, paying not with their money but with a different asset: their attention. That resulted in a shift in power from the old gatekeepers of media who controlled content creation and distribution—the publishers, record labels, and movie studios—to those platforms who amassed consumer attention at scale.

With value exchange baked into the core of Web 3.0 through the blockchain and cryptocurrency, it opens new opportunities for content creators;

- Tokens: Blockchain-based smart contracts have created new currencies and new opportunities. Content creators can now be empowered by a type of cryptocurrency called 'social tokens'. Creative folk can essentially issue a currency tied to their community.

- Monetisation: Social tokens enable creators to build and reward their community and compensate themselves. This option creates something far better than "likes" for creators – actual money. Now, creators don't have to rely on ads to monetise their content; they can monetise directly and indirectly from their audience donating coins to them.

- Finance: Creators can be paid in real time, with royalties flowing directly to digital wallets. And through Non Fungible Tokens (NFTs), creators can even be paid on the secondary sales of content.

We are at the early stages of Web 3.0 and so much is yet to become clear. One thing is abundantly clear however, Web 3.0 is the future of the internet and we are at the perfect moment to begin thinking about how we can capitalise on this opportunity.

CUSTOMER
CONTEXT
CREATIVITY
COMMUNITY
CHANNELS
CALCULATION

CHAPTER 17
EARNED AND PAID CHANNELS. MAXIMISING GROWTH THROUGH ADVOCACY AND PAID MEDIA

I'm often surprised by the number of well-structured content plans I see that miss out on a key component; promotion.

For any content we create, we need to consider how we will maximise the value of the effort we spent creating it. To do this, start by asking yourself these questions, which will encourage you to think beyond just publishing to your 'owned' social channels;

- What influencers and creators could we collaborate with that will help us reach more of our target audience?
- Which of our employees' personal profiles could we share this content to to maximise reach?
- How can we encourage audience participation on our content?
- What communities and groups could help us promote and share this content?
- What budgets should we apply to this content to maximise its chances of success?
- What media outlets could we collaborate with to help us share this content?

To ensure maximum distribution of your content, we need to consider the concept of 'Paid, Owned and Earned'.

We've covered 'earned' media through the 'Community' step and 'owned' media in the previous chapter, so now let's turn our attention to 'paid' media.

There are a number of paid media opportunities that we have outside of social, like Google PPC, sponsorships, Display ads and retargeting, but for the purpose of 'Social 3.0', we are going to focus our attention on paid social.

There are however two challenges facing all paid social media strategies;

1. Reducing impact

As we shared earlier, 47% of internet users now use ad blockers and Apple's iOS 14.5 privacy update has resulted in 96% of users opting out of Facebook tracking their usage behaviours. This means that our typical 'go-to' paid social platform, Facebook is not going to deliver the precise targeting it once did.

2. **Rising costs**

As a result of the above, we've seen some worrying statistics that point to a continually reducing ROAS (Return On Advertising Spend). Emplify suggests that Facebook and Instagram ad spend increased by 43% between Q3 2019 and Q3 2021. This increase in competition naturally pushes up prices. As a result the Cost per Click (CPC) nearly doubled between August 2020 and August 2021. The kicker however is that Click-through Rates (CTR) decreased by 10% over the same period. [56]

This means that we need to re-think our approach if we are to outsmart the competition and realise the true potential of paid social media content.

The first thing that's required is a mindset shift. Most brands think of paid social in the same way as they do Google PPC, forgetting there's a big difference between

---

[56] https://go.emplifi.io/rs/284-ENW-442/images/Emplifi%20-%20Report%20-%20Social%20Media%20and%20CX%20Trends%20Q3%202021_EN.pdf

demand capture and *demand creation*. This misunderstanding results in a high cost per lead (CPL), poor lead quality and inordinately high cost of customer acquisition.

We need to think of paid social as *demand creation* rather than *demand capture*. Let's look at the differences.

Demand capture

The best places to capture demand are where buyers go when they are in buying mode: Examples include:

- Google search (paid & organic)
  - When it comes to search, look for clear signals for purchase intent. For example:
  - Good: "Best social media management software"
  - Bad: "What is social media management software"
- Review sites (e.g. G2, TrustRadius, etc.)
- Affiliates (e.g. Software Advice, Affiliate blogs, etc.)

Demand creation

As with everything we produce on social media, we need to think 'audience-first'. We need to realise that whilst social media represents the 3rd highest source of brand discovery, 95% of your audience are not in the market to buy.

It's also very unlikely you'll hit the remaining 5% that are in the market for your product regularly, especially in light of ever-reducing targeting fidelity. And no one wants to create a strategy based on chance.

That's when we need to re-categorise paid social in our mind as *demand creation*, not *demand capture*. That means optimising our content for consumption in the feed. It means serving content that is focussed on what the audience are interested in and likely to engage with — meaning we need to think beyond the landing page.

Why? Data from one of my favourite B2B marketers, Chris Walker suggests that the average click-through rate on LinkedIn ads is 0.4%.[57] As marketers, we obsess over

[57] https://www.linkedin.com/posts/chris-walker-41597028_marketing-gotomarket-b2b-activity-6901887443675561984-gQ33

our landing pages and data capture fields, but we're missing the point — most people never click.

Here's a new strategy for paid social

We need to apply the SOCIAL 3.0 framework to our paid content. If we truly understand our audience, we'll know the story we need to tell. If we know the story we need to tell, we can focus our creative efforts on how we tell this story in a way that our targets will actually care about. (Because we've taken the time to understand them)

If over 99% of people never click, we need to educate, inform or entertain our audience **in the feed**. However, as this approach to paid social has now become a 'brand-building' endeavour that focuses on awareness and demand creation, it's going to be a tough pill to swallow for some marketing and leadership teams, as we won't be able to measure with such binary numbers, like number of leads generated.

It means we need a new model for evaluating success. Typical attribution models won't work here. If we are trying to tie social media performance (both organic and paid) to sales, we are on a road to nowhere. This is what's been holding B2B's back from unleashing the potential of social. Metrics and goals drive behaviours, so if we only care about the sales we attribute to social, marketing teams will continue to churn out ads that get some short term conversions, but do so at the expense of the long term performance of the brand.

Social media's superpower is in lighting a fire under word of mouth. Our content needs to be optimised to get people talking and sharing (using all of the learnings we shared in the Creativity, Community and Channels steps).

For example, if you created a social ad that was a short video shot with a recognised and respected individual within your category that spoke to a real challenge your target audience faces and did it in a way that encouraged interaction, I'll bet my house you'll see better results than a conversion-focussed ad that was optimised on driving clicks to yet another whitepaper.

B2B's have gotten lazy. They are using social ads as a 'set it and forget it' channel, thinking that they are targeting a pool of buyers that are waiting for them. As we know, that's just not the case and as the social ads market continues to get flooded with new advertisers, this really is the time we pivot our approach.

Let's be honest, buying ads is easy. What most B2B marketers haven't figured out yet is how to use social ads to tell a story that drives business outcomes.

However, that won't be the case for you. The SOCIAL 3.0 framework will save your business from ending up like most B2B's. You'll be thinking audience-first, telling a story that your audience cares about and it'll be a story that's intrinsically linked to the change you seek to make.

This approach will require us to be smarter with how we measure success and importantly, how we tell this story internally with our businesses so that we can take them on a journey of understanding the true impact of social media.

With that, let's begin the final chapter and the last step of the SOCIAL 3.0 framework.

CUSTOMER

CONTEXT

CREATIVITY

COMMUNITY

CHANNELS

CALCULATION

CHAPTER 18

CALCULATION.

EVALUATING AND TRACKING

SUCCESS

Let's start by making one thing crystal clear. B2B's need to change how they measure social media performance. The typical approach to attribution and the desire to draw a simple line between content and conversion kills creativity and stunts innovation.

We need to embrace the fact that leveraging the influential power of social media means that whilst we have the opportunity to generate awareness, build trust, create communities, maximise mental availability and foster word of mouth at scale we don't have an easy way to measure it.

As we've already seen through this book, social media impacts all areas of your business, from insights and discovery to conversion and advocacy and trying to quantify all of this impact in a spreadsheet is a massive waste of time.

From a sales perspective, it's pretty obvious the ads are working when your target audience are requesting demos saying they heard about your company on social media. It's not complicated. Just make it a practice for your sales team to ask each customer how they heard about you and ensure that's recorded in your CRM. Make that part of your process and you'll have more accurate data than 90% of B2B's that have invested in expensive marketing attribution software that they spend all of their days trying to fix issues with.

Marketers have become increasingly fixated on data. But data on its own misses the important nuance. Like we discussed earlier, data is nothing without a story and one single conversation with one single customer can lead to more breakthroughs than a day spent staring at a Google Analytics dashboard.

That said, there are useful insights or 'metrics that matter' we need to gather to help us understand if we are achieving the right results.

Going back to the SOCIAL 3.0 Framework, having set our objectives at step 5, we need to evaluate our performance against them in this final step, which will help inform the content we will create for the next cycle.

SOCIAL 3.0 FRAMEWORK

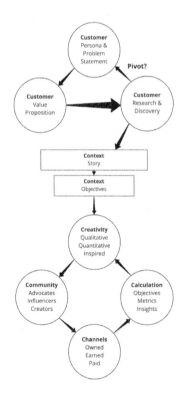

Returning back to our 'objective setting' stage at step 5, we need to evaluate our performance against what we were looking to achieve with our strategy.

As you'll recall, there are really only five things that we're ever out to achieve.

For example,

- **Awareness**
We're seeking to get our messages and brand seen by as many people as possible.

- **Consideration**
We're seeking to build trust and affinity with our audience

- **Conversion**
We're seeking for someone to take action

- **Loyalty**
We're trying to make people love us and stay with us

- **Advocacy**
We're trying to make our offering so powerful that it benefits our audience to tell others.

Let's go back to the example objective we used earlier of' *'become number one in the market.* We had established that the first step in becoming 'number one' is always going to be about getting in front of more people and as a result, increasing our share of voice.

We would have benchmarked our share of voice in the objective setting stage, so all we need to do is go back to the tool we used to calculate this (in this case www.mentionlytics.com) and evaluate the growth over this period.

Talking of reporting periods, I'd suggest at a maximum reporting monthly, ideally quarterly. The longer the reporting period, the richer the learnings and the less time is wasted on actions that don't directly benefit your audience.

In addition to share of voice, I'd recommend evaluating 'impression' growth over the same period (the total number of times your content was shown). The 'impressions' metric is one that's available across all social channels, both paid and organic, so it provides for a simple, consistent and comparative metric to track your growth across all channels.

These two metrics will give you a simple picture of whether you are making progress towards your objective and should form the basis of your strategic reporting.

To optimise for the next cycle, I would recommend going deeper to understand impression growth at a content level, which will help you identify what content has driven your growth and what content did not perform as expected.

In the objective setting stage, we would have benchmarked the baseline number of impressions we receive per post across each channel. From this we know that we are looking for an improvement in the average number of impressions per post. To do this, we simply look into our social media post level analytics for both paid and organic content (we can do this on the platforms themselves, or use a social media analytics tool to save time) and look at those posts that have performed better than the baseline. We then take this top performing content and save it back to our 'library of inspiration' we discussed in the 'quantitative creativity' step to build on in the next cycle.

This is a key part of the SOCIAL 3.0 Framework; Setting clear business-level objectives, aligning on the *'metrics that matter'*, then evaluating your success against these metrics and using the results to inform your learnings and future content plan.

I would also recommend going one final dimension deeper in post-level analysis and look at 'engagement rate'. Engagement rate is the measure of the percentage of '*interactions*' (likes, comments, shares, clicks etc.) per every 100 impressions. For example, if your post was seen 100 times (100 'impressions') and received 10 interactions (the total number of likes, comments or shares), it would give you an engagement rate of 10%. Throughout the course of this book, we've spoken about being 'audience-first' and telling a story that they care about. We've also shared the importance of encouraging audience participation on your content. Remember, the more your content is engaged with, the more it will be shown in the feed.

As a result, engagement drives impression growth and as such, you should see your 'engagement rate' as your 'content quality score'. In any type of analysis, it's better to think in terms of ratios and percentages rather than absolute numbers, as this is a better way to understand underlying performance. Again, as with our impression analysis, we go into our post-level performance and evaluate which posts have performed above our baseline in terms of engagement rate and we take those top performing posts back into our 'library of inspiration' to evolve and repurpose in the next content cycle.

Of course, whilst we have focussed on the 'top of funnel' for this example, we want to demonstrate that we need to focus our analysis on the key areas of the business we want to impact, which in this example was the 'awareness' stage.

As we've already mentioned, social media impacts all areas of the business and the marketing funnel. As a result, it can be tempting to measure everything, but it's just not practical. The key to most things in life and business is focus. Once you have aligned with the leadership team on the impact you want to make, that becomes your objective and the metrics and measures should focus only on that.

My recommendation? Push heavily against any objective that focuses too far down the funnel as then we are constricting and limiting the impact of the influential power of social media.

Connecting solid research to a consistent workflow, and backing that up with actionable data, creates a process that generates predictable, reliable and scalable content marketing results.

Remember that mindset shift we spoke about? That we need to think of social media (both paid and organic) as *demand creation* as opposed to *demand capture?*

Well, any business that wants to unlock the opportunity of SOCIAL 3.0, needs to have a look at the example below as a cautionary tale. Taking this short-term led mindset will lead to high customer acquisition costs, slower than expected growth and will ultimately result in limited business valuations.

In the words of Social media consultant, Tamasine McCaig [58]; *'The work I have done with B2B brands has taught me is the importance of relationships on social media.*

I therefore find it amazing how often B2B brands and organisations try to deliver social media but don't think through the whole of the relationship. It's very often a tick box exercise and they focus too strongly on ROI alone.

In a number of cases I worked on B2B projects, (often involving LinkedIn) where I would establish and train and set up programmes to build staff as Thought Leaders. They start off keen, often having been asked by someone else in the business to be THE FACE of

---

[58] https://www.linkedin.com/in/tamasinemcaig/

the brand on LinkedIn. Just as they just start to find their feet, the marketing budget has been cut - they've been told hat there haven't been enough sales that can be linked to the profile growth. The finance team, or the person comparing it to CTR on Google wants instant results.

I always remain calm, try to explain that it can't just be about ROI - and that they need to ask themselves if you can really put a financial value on a relationship? Nothing may come of that relationship for many years, but you have to nurture any relationship for it to grow.'

Jess, who worked in social media in B2B corporates for a number of years;

'Social media is seen as a nice to have, even an 'extra-curricular' some might say. But as any credible marketer knows, this is far from the case.

Similarly to Tamasine, I've been running projects with the aim of profiling our subject-matter experts in the business as external thought leaders on LinkedIn, and some have been a lot more receptive than others. As the saying goes, you can lead the horse to water but you can't make it drink! Sometimes it takes that lightbulb moment for them to see its worth - whether it's a post from an ex-colleague or a post of their own that has seen great engagement. But once that spark has lit, the opportunities are endless.

Even in 2022, with social media's popularity growing, I often feel a sense of dread when people ask me what I do as a job... "Oh, so you post on LinkedIn?". There is a strong generational divide that comes with deeply ingrained thoughts and views on the digital space as a whole, and as a social media manager, this makes the hurdles never ending.

There are few other ways you can directly target your buying committee than social media: PPC is luck of the draw, SEO sees you constantly chasing to understand the latest algorithm update and email is reliant on having up-to-date data. Whilst social media does take an investment from both time and monetary perspective, there is no price you can put on relationship building, community growth, and as the title of the book goes, 'the power of trust'.

Consumers expect so much more from companies now, and this has grown exponentially as a result of the pandemic.

The new(ish) buzzword we all see floating around at the moment is 'humanizing' B2B, but in my own opinion this isn't something that shouldn't be a trend, rather something that should've been part of the strategy since day 0. We need to overcome the misconception that B2B content has to be monotonous. Influencers are now badged as creators and this is going to drive branded B2B content – the halo effect of brands focusing on working with creators on social media in the next year will be like none other.

Social media and the digital space as a whole for brands is following the steps of natural selection. Evolve to stay relevant by keeping up with the trends such as new channels, new ad formats or even the likes of the unknown opportunities in Web3 and the Metaverse, or be left behind and lose your digital real estate, and therefore your customers.'

Tamasine and Jess sum up perfectly the opportunity and risks that face B2B businesses. The fastest-growing and most-loved businesses on the planet all have realised the transformative potential of social media, but it's opening up a great divide between those that 'get it' and those that are still marketing like it's 2012.

B2B's, it's time to cross the chasm to unleash the power of social media, to build trust and create demand at a scale that's never before been possible.

Printed in Great Britain
by Amazon